CERAMIC COIN BANKS

Identification & Value Guide

Tom & Loretta Stoddard

COLLECTOR BOOKS

A Division of Schroeder Publishing Co., Inc.

The current values in this book should be used only as a guide. They are not intended to set prices, which vary from one section of the country to another. Auction prices as well as dealer prices vary greatly and are affected by condition as well as demand. Neither the Authors nor the Publisher assumes responsibility for any losses that might be incurred as a result of consulting this guide.

Searching For A Publisher?

We are always looking for knowledgeable people considered to be experts within their fields. If you feel that there is a real need for a book on your collectible subject and have a large comprehensive collection, contact Collector Books.

On the cover, left to right:

Flowered cat, #287, redware pottery, c1900, Swiss Thume folkware, 3⅜"h, note edelweiss on rear leg identifying it as Swiss, E; $400.00 – 500.00.

Girl on bed, #257, porcelain, c1910, German, 2½"h, 1557 incised on foot of bed; D; $300.00 – 350.00.

Boxer head, #306, pottery, 1880 – 1900, English-Staffordshire, 2"h, C; $250.00 – 300.00.

Girl in sunsuit with umbrella, #192, porcelain, c1935, Japan, 3⅝"h, D; $225.00 – 275.00.

Auto, #884, pottery with lusterware drip glaze, c1935, US, 2⅛"h, D; $200.00 – 250.00.

Cover Design: Beth Summers
Book Design: Benjamin R. Faust

Contents

Acknowledgments

Several people helped on this book above and beyond the call. They were Lester Breininger for writing the material for American folkart redware banks, Sidney Gecker of American Folk Art for providing American folkart redware bank photos and data, Brian Cleary who read and corrected the manuscript more times than we have, Don Duer who provided a substantial part of the photographs from his collection and others, and Fred Cox, M.D., who helped review the manuscript and provided useful data.

We are also appreciative of Lisa Stroup of Collector Books for her helpful suggestions and Schroeder Publishing Co, Inc. for publishing this work.

Many thanks to the following people who helped us complete this book:

Norm Bowers
Ralph Crawford, Jr.
Ralph Dye, Jr.
Betty Hale
Mike Henry
Mrs. G. Robert "Kax" Herberger
Tom Kellogg
Christine MacKenzie
Gary Stradling

and, of course, Nell Vanderhoef, Tom's mom, and Helen McMurtrey, Loretta's mom.

Introduction

It is not necessary to read or own this book to enjoy collecting and appreciating ceramic coin banks. One of the most stalwart ceramic bank collectors, Ralph Dye, put it best, "I don't know much about who made them, or where they came from, or even when they were made; they're just so beautiful — I love to collect and admire them." Ralph is, however, expected at the head of the line to buy this book, and we know he will be delighted with every detail of discovery. Importantly, this book can prevent both the novice and advanced collector from making purchasing errors, and the avoidance of only one such error can easily pay for the book. This book should also add substantial texture and depth to ceramic bank collecting, thus adding immeasurably to our general collecting pleasure. In addition, it fills the human need to know.

The task of compiling a ceramic bank book has been approached a step at a time, thus making what once seemed overwhelming now possible. Such a pioneering work cannot pretend to be complete, but it can bring a rich pattern of detail heretofore missing from this field of collecting. Here presented is a structure and broad outline within which future researcher-authors and/or future revisions can fill in some of the blanks and answer unanswered questions. Every time a new piece of information is discovered, it confirms that there exists someone, somewhere who can fill a blank.

The term ceramic is used to describe all fired products containing some earth-mined clays. The two major ceramic divisions are earthenware and porcelain. Earthenware is generally divided into pottery and stoneware, while porcelain divides into three types: hard paste or true porcelain, artificial (or soft), and bone china. The technical refinements among these divisions are daunting, and only the most dedicated student will want to explore them in detail. Ceramics does not include chalkware, a material excluded from this volume. Chalkware is plaster of Paris which is produced by adding water to calcinated gypsum and allowing it to harden. It is often used as molds for producing ceramics. While chalkware and ceramics have some similar characteristics, the essential process of heating is absent from chalkware.

This book covers pre-WWII coin banks with one small fudge; we have included the charming ceramic banks of Occupied Japan and they are so identified. The pre-WWII period covers the major collecting and research interest of most collectors. It is a handy point for dividing styles and manufacturers, and it has been used by numerous researcher-authors as a convenient dividing point. After WWII some countries ceased to exist, some changed their names, and many manufacturers disappeared completely. Germany became East and West Germany. Japan marked products "Made In Occupied Japan" from 1945 to 1952. The world divided into East and West with only modest trade between

them for years afterward and the ceramic centers of Eastern Europe sent nothing westward until the 1980s.

This book is in color because much of the charm of ceramic banks is their gorgeous colors and glazes. The colors and glazes are the result of many millenniums of thought, experimentation, and practice. At "The Potteries" in England you can enter a ceramic coloring room where various ingredients for colors and glazes are stored. There are hundreds of different ingredients and thousands of different combinations in a modern ceramic manufacturing plant which can produce an almost limitless variety of finishes.

The arrangement of this book could follow a number of paths such as chronological, alphabetical, geographical, types of ceramics, manufacturers, or subject. The decision to arrange the photographs by subject is primarily for ease in finding a particular bank. If it is a pig, then looking under pigs is easier than trying to identify the manufacturer or finding it in a necessarily flawed chronology. This method also follows the Whiting, Moore, and Long-Pitman methods of still bank books and will, therefore, be familiar to still bank collectors. Other ceramic collectors and readers should also find it easy to use.

Several subjects will be covered before the main body of the book is presented. These subjects are manufacturing processes, identification and dating, condition, prices, and ratings. This is followed by text broken down by geography (US, Japan, Germany, etc.) with specific locations (Bennington, Vt.; Bohemia; etc.) under the country and then manufacturers (Roseville, Schafer & Vater, George Ohr, etc.) under these locations. Because of the unknown nature about much of the subject, unknown material is grouped under best guess location followed by a parenthetical question mark (?) or, if even a guess is not justified, left blank. Each ceramic piece is numbered, showing its material, age, country, manufacturer, height, rarity and approximate value, and any manufacturer's marks or other comments.

One of the perplexing and interesting aspects of collecting ceramic coin banks is the never ending diversity of the subject. It is already established that ceramic coin banks will outnumber those of any other pre-WWII material. The experienced coin bank collector will discover, as we have, that the rarity ratings are spread much differently than those of other materials. Exploring the diverse avenues opened by ceramic banks also opens new avenues and other possibilities for learning, exploration, and enrichment. It reinforces the notion of the more you know, the more you know you don't know.

Another perplexing dilemma in reading and researching ceramic coin banks is the reluctance of authors to identify coin banks. One Staffordshire book identifies a number of pastille burners side by side with a number of banks and tells us items three, five, and six are pastille burners but doesn't mention money boxes or coin banks. In a majolica book many items are identified, but no coin banks are shown. Only a few books mention coin banks, money boxes, penny banks, money jugs, banks, or savings banks. When researching ceramic coin banks, look at the illustrations in addition to the index to see if any banks are presented.

Ceramics is one of the oldest man-made products, emerging shortly after the Stone Age about 10,000 years ago. There is only one essential process for producing ceramics — heating clay to at least 800°F. The second oldest process, almost contemporary with firing, is decorating the clay before or after it's fired. The third part of the process, glazing, began about the same time and gives ceramics a pro-

tective coating. No matter how complex these processes become, these three fundamental processes underlie the production of a ceramic: firing, decorating, and glazing.

In the interest of continued research and a possible future revised edition, commentary, corrections, and additions are encouraged. Those with information please write to Tom and Loretta Stoddard at PO Box 71, Petaluma, CA 94953. Please do not telephone since it is difficult to record information and get the complete story this way. Please write out whatever information you have from as many sources as possible, including title pages of books, tables of contents, and/or covers of magazines. Photocopy them and forward them with your suggestions and comments.

Thanks,

Tom & Loretta

Ceramic Manufacturing Process

The process for ceramic manufacture was discovered by man about 10,000 years ago and has been growing in quantity and quality steadily since then. Today even space travel relies on ceramics. There is only one essential process to producing ceramics: heating clay to 800°F or higher. As clay is heated it permanently hardens, and even though shielding tiles for spacecraft are super heated in highly sophisticated ovens, the basic process is still the same as it was in the Stone Age. The first ceramics were probably heated at the fireside. After that it took only a modest intellectual leap to realize heating them in or by fire was faster and resulted in a stronger, less porous product. Gener-

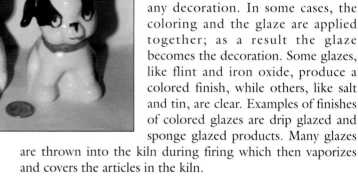

ally, the hotter the clay is heated the harder and less permeable the finished product. There are, of course, a few exceptions and many technical nuances.

Following the production of simple clay products the process of decoration began. Decorating is done either by painting with various pigments, including glazing material, or applying different colored clays on or fused in the product. Thus, the second oldest ceramic process began, almost contemporaneously with firing, that of decorating the clay before or after its firing.

The third part of the process, glazing, began about the same time. Glazing was discovered more or less simultane-

ously in ancient Egypt, China, Assyria, and Babylon. Glazing is a liquid or powder applied to the ceramic piece that, after firing, gives the ceramic a hard vitreous finish. In most cases, the glazing produces a kind of glass covering, making the piece more durable, waterproof, and attractive. Glazing stops most of the porosity, protects the fired body, and preserves any decoration. In some cases, the coloring and the glaze are applied together; as a result the glaze becomes the decoration. Some glazes, like flint and iron oxide, produce a colored finish, while others, like salt and tin, are clear. Examples of finishes of colored glazes are drip glazed and sponge glazed products. Many glazes are thrown into the kiln during firing which then vaporizes and covers the articles in the kiln.

No matter how complex the process becomes, these three fundamental processes underlie the product: firing, decorating and glazing. As mentioned, of the three, only heating is essential. Firing, by the way, reduces the size of the green ceramic or clay by about 17 percent.

Ceramic manufacturers were great copyists. Not only did they copy other ceramic manufacturers, they copied nearly anything they thought might sell. The examples shown above and on the following page, the cast-iron American made "Fido" bank copied in porcelain by a Japanese manufacturer possibly using the original for a mold, and a Japanese lead bust bank copied in porcelain by another Japanese manufacturer, are only two of many examples.

Ceramic describes all products containing some earth-mined clays. The two big divisions are earthenware and porcelain.

Earthenware contains primarily earth-mined clays and is further divided into pottery and stoneware.

Pottery is heated earth-mined clay ranging from fire heated to kiln heated. Redware is one of the common types of pottery.

Stoneware is made of clay and fusible stone usually heated above 1000°F. There are several sub-categories which are of little interest since there are few stoneware banks.

Pottery is low-fired clay that fuses at the particle edges at about 800°F. It is porous and requires glazing to make it waterproof. Stoneware can be nearly translucent but is usually made so thick it is not. It does contain some fusible mineral like porcelain but has a larger proportion of clay and is not fired as hot as porcelain, usually about 1000°F. Pottery scratches fairly easily while stoneware is very hard to scratch. Test scratching in an unimportant location with a knife will usually tell whether a piece is pottery or stoneware.

Majolica is one of the most collected and appreciated of the earthenware potteries and is an anglicized version of the Italian. It is called Maiolica (in Italy where it originated), or Delftware (Holland), or faience (France), mezza-majolica, and raffaele ware (England). Majolica was adopted as a trade name by Minton in the Staffordshire area. Majolica is a tin-glazed finish resulting in a bright and colorful earthenware. Some of the most interesting and sought-after pieces of majolica are a number of bust banks made in Czechoslovakia between 1919 and 1940, see #2 through #38.

Porcelain is translucent and/or gives a ringing note when struck. There are three general types: hard paste, soft paste (or artificial china), and bone china. Porcelain is made by combining fusible minerals, usually feldspar, with clay and heating to over 1200°F. There are a daunting number of technical refinements and nuances among various divisions and only the most dedicated student will want to explore them in detail.

Hard paste porcelain, a true porcelain, contains white refractory clay or kaolin and feldspathic rock. It fuses at over 1450°F.

Artificial porcelain, or soft paste porcelain, is made using powdered glass instead of feldspathic rock to create the translucency and is fused at 1200°F.

Bone china porcelain, a true porcelain, adds bone ash obtained from animal bones which improves the fusion of the ingredients and is otherwise like hard paste porcelain.

> EXTRA: The term "piggy bank" is often ascribed to potters who call the raw clay "pig." Early banks were simple clay jugs or pots made from raw clay or pig and were thus called piggy banks. Eventually they were made in the actual pig shape. Another reported origin of piggy bank is that pigs are a symbol of fecundity in many cultures. To symbolize that savings would grow, early potters began making banks in the rough shape of pigs. Over the years the pigs became more detailed and today hundreds of different shapes abound.

The quickest and easiest way to tell earthenware from porcelain is to see if light shines through it. In most cases, light will shine through porcelain but not through earthenware. The coin slot of a coin bank offers a convenient opening to put the eye to while holding the rest of the piece up to the light or sun. Only very thick porcelain will not let the light through; but since the object of porcelain is to be thin, translucent, and elegant, thick porcelain is a contradiction in purpose and is very unusual. The very thinnest porcelain is called eggshell porcelain; it is made so thin it resembles the thickness and translucency of eggshells. The Chinese in the Ming dynasty called it "bodiless porcelain."

Ceramics does not include chalkware and it is not covered in this volume. Chalkware, also known as plaster of Paris, a soft usually white material, is produced by adding water to calcinated gypsum and allowing it to harden. It is often used as molds for producing ceramics. While chalkware and ceramics have some similar characteristics the essential process of heating or firing is absent in chalkware. Carnival doll prizes are made of chalkware.

Jasperware (invented by Sir Thomas Wedgwood and often called Wedgwood) is a form of stoneware. Jasperware has been made by many companies besides Wedgwood since its introduction in 1774. There are several jasperware banks that date from around the turn of the century. Two seen most often are a teapot and sugar bowl included in the photographic section. They are European in origin and both have washed tin tops and bottoms, neither is Wedgwood. Wedgwood made its first jasperware coin bank in the 1960s to celebrate its two-hundredth year in business.

The process of shaping the clay is done in three principal ways: molding with the hands; turning on a wheel using the hands or jig-type devices to shape the cylinder as it rotates; and placing the clay in a mold. Again, each of these processes can become incredibly complex, as anyone who has visited a major ceramics factory can attest. While most modern ceramics production uses molds, some production uses a bit of all three methods.

Hand molding is the oldest method and the one we learned in kindergarten when we were given a lump of clay from the always damp and heavily lidded stoneware pot. Often one of the first steps is to roll the clay into rope-like strands and then coil them together to begin the piece. Hand molding is still used to create most art ceramics, to create fine finish details for expensive pieces, to create weird and exotic shapes, or to create one-of-a-kind pieces.

Wheel-turned pottery is done on a potter's wheel. Nearly everyone has watched a potter in action, fascinated with the changing cylinder as the potter works. The history and changes of the wheel alone would make an interesting volume.

Mold Process: Mold-made banks are produced by making a master mold. The master mold is then used to make 15 to 25 molds. Each mold is in turn used to make 20 to 50 banks. The reason the master molds and the molds wear out is they lose detail as the subtle crevices are filled with raw clay and then reused.

The first mold from the master mold used to make the first bank will be a far superior product than the twenty-fifth mold made from the master mold used to make the fiftieth bank. As detail is lost, so is desirability and value. Some manufacturers were fairly careful to give full detail for the dollar, others cared only that it could be used for a bank. Several examples illustrated have lost so much detail they cannot be definitely identified as to the subject. Is it a bear or a pig? Is it a lion or cat?

There are two types of molds, press molds and drain molds. In the former, the clay is pressed inside two or more incus hollows. The molded pieces are removed and then joined until sufficiently dry. After that they are cleaned and

fired. The cleaning entails removing bits of excess material particularly at the joining seams. The joining seam is where the molded parts are joined together leaving a seam. In some cases it is almost impossible to find the exact location of the seam, and in others, it is almost impossible not to notice it. Generally, the joining seam is visible in proportion to the relative sales price of the piece; the higher the price, the less visible. With a drain mold, the parts are joined together before the liquid clay is poured in. After it hardens, usually speeded by adding a chemical, the mold is removed, the seams cleaned, and the piece fired.

EXTRA: Potter's field — most potters were near the bottom of the skill ladder and often wandered the countryside looking for low-pay piecework. The work consisted mostly of working a wheel repetitiously producing pots, plates, and bowls. When a potter died he rarely left burial funds. Penniless, he was buried in the unmarked section of the local graveyard, which, because it received so many potters, became known as the potter's field.

Some commentators on ceramic coin banks have theorized that the size of the coin slot is indicative of age. The smaller the slot the older the bank. Here we show two examples of the same bank with different size coin slots. The slots vary by six or seven multiples in both banks. Note the irregular shape of the cat on the right. Since slots were not molded into the bank, but hand cut after the unfired piece was taken from the mold, it shows a more human tendency to expand and contract and wander around.

This text tries to keep the amount of knowledge needed to understand and appreciate the making and collecting of ceramic coin banks within manageable portions and understandable compartments. And, while much more knowledge is available about ceramic history, production, and makers, it is left to the readers to delve further into the subject as their interests lead them. Those wanting additional reading are referred to the bibliography. Particularly recommended is, *An Illustrated Dictionary of Ceramics* (3,054 terms relating to wares, materials, processes, styles, patterns, and shapes from antiquity to the present day).

Identification and Dating

The ceramic coin banks which have been identified by country, manufacturer, and approximate dates are referred to as "known" banks. The serious problem comes in identifying and dating banks not falling into the categories of known banks. It is difficult, impossible in many cases, to determine their country of origin, manufacturer, and/or approximate date of production. Even when they are known, they are sometimes erroneously known, as in the next paragraph, and, therefore, just as mysterious as if nothing were known. Developing the barest information on unknown banks is a serious challenge and the attribution is tentative based on information at hand. Where they are tentatively identified they are followed by (?).

There are a number of books published which have errors in them. One Roseville pottery book shows a number of McCoy pigs as being made by Roseville. The identification of those pigs in this volume is correct. Another book shows Greenville cottages as being Staffordshire. While they are similar, there are important differences and, again, see the Greenville identification for the correct one. Similarly, serious mistakes have been discovered in museums, not the least of which was several so-called Bennington coin banks at the Bennington Museum, Bennington, Vermont, which have proven not to be from either the Fenton or Norton potteries of Bennington, Vermont.

It is still not clear whether the famous porcelain maker Royal Bayreuth made coin banks. If they did, they were unmarked because no Royal Bayreuth mark (an elaborate coat of arms) has been found on a coin bank. Royal Bayreuth, according to some experts, always marked their pieces. Others say, "Not so!" They contend that Royal Bayreuth did not mark their cheap lines, such as coin banks. Others contend a careful examination of the similar but unmarked pieces shows they do not have the uniformity of high-quality underpaint or glaze of Royal Bayreuth. This volume avoids the controversy and does not identify any banks as made by Royal Bayreuth.

Any research, such as we have here, is confronted with the confusion of history (necessarily confused because it is

only partially and erratically recorded and, even then, usually long after the historical event), confusion of ignorance, and confusion by design, and the daunting task of trying to separate one from the other.

For several areas of confusion, take the Roseville Pottery Company, begun in Roseville, Ohio, in 1885. In 1902 they expanded to Zanesville, Ohio, where most of their subsequent manufacturing took place. They had many lines of pottery with many names; one, combining their two locations, was called Rozane. Rookwood Pottery Company was founded in 1879 in Cincinnati, Ohio, and became the number one art potter of America. Rookwood's lines were imitated by Roseville in Zanesville (there are no known Rookwood still banks). J. W. McCoy Pottery Company was founded in 1899 in Roseville, Ohio, and became the Brush-McCoy Pottery Company in 1910, and then the Brush Pottery Company in 1925. Meanwhile, Nelson, the son of J. W. McCoy, founded the Nelson McCoy Sanitary Stoneware Company in Roseville. Finally, to further confuse the public, the Brush-McCoy Company made an art pottery line called Rosewood (probably combining the names ROSEville and RookWOOD). The result was easily confused with Rozane, Roseville, or Rookwood. There are McCoy (Brush-McCoy) and Roseville banks. There are multi-volume books on Roseville, Rookwood, and McCoy potteries, most of which illustrate no banks.

It is easy to be confused by various experts on various levels who propound various statements and theories as illustrated above. We are sure there will be confusion arising from this volume which, while unintentional, will require a future revision. Also, as every collector knows, the imagination of antique dealers is very fecund. While we get much useful information, we also get a lot of fertilizer, and buyers are advised to verify any sales pitch information. Here the information is usually verified from two sources, but it is still subject to errors, omissions, unproven theories, and speculation, and corrections of any errant material is encouraged.

In a few rare instances, coin bank makers conveniently dated their work by coloring, incising, or slip decorating the date. Most of these are presentation banks or banks made to be presented to someone at Christmas, on a birthday, or other special event. Examples of these are #1, #822, and #838. These gifts were often made by potters who inscribed the names of presenter and/or presentee and often the date. For a gift giver/potter it solved a problem of giving a thoughtful yet affordable gift. Of course, this assumes these banks were actually made when stated. This then is the best date, permanently affixed and immutable. However, nothing prevents the unscrupulous from making a bank today and dating it 1851. In these instances it is best to know the provenance or pedigree of the bank. This means where it's been in the ensuing years and any records to substantiate its whereabouts. Because the coin bank was considered an inconsequential item, few records exist.

One example of provenance are ceramic banks from the Dr. Arthur E. Corby, DDS, bank collection. Corby was an early ceramic bank collector who died in 1954. He wrote his name on the bottom of his ceramic banks. Being an early collector, Corby had no reason to deceive and his marked banks predate 1954. His banks have since scattered to about a dozen collectors including our collection. Another example is the Norton bank from the Norton Pottery in Bennington, Vermont, which was in the Norton family until removed to the Bennington Museum. It is also dated. Still another is the Seaman Bank collection sold at auction by Christie's in March 1991. Each of their pieces had a purple-brown paint stripe with white numbers on it, and banks conforming to that identification were in the Seaman Bank Collection.

Some European makers, notably the Austria-Bohemia-Czechoslovakia and German potteries, have pattern numbers incised on the bottom or written under the glaze on the back of them. These sometimes conform to calendar dates, like 1921 or 1913, but are not really dates of manufacture. The number probably indicates the sequence in which the banks began manufacture but, since they would be discontinued based on their sales popularity, their ending date and life span would be unknown.

A few banks have notations written on the bottom in pen or pencil. While this is a somewhat unreliable method for obvious reasons, it is often a clue and when combined with other observations can be very useful. The inscription is usually like, "To Timmie on his sixth birthday, June 1, 1906." Or, "Received on Aug 11, 1889, on my sixth birthday." Occasionally such data will be on a paste-on label. Sometimes the labels will have data from former owners, "Found at Spottswood, Pa, April 1955." Or, "Seller said made about 1900 at Bangor, Maine."

Another method of identification is by documentation. This can be an old letter accompanying the piece, a note attached to the gift, a diary page noting its arrival, a catalog, an advertisement, or salesman's literature. Catalogs and advertisements are an excellent method of dating. Unfortunately,

few catalogs or advertisements exist for ceramic coin banks. The only one known, an early Roseville advertisement seeking salesmen for their early line of pottery fruit banks, is shown in the Huxford's *Collector's Encyclopedia Of Roseville Pottery*. We expect that a few others may surface with the publication of this book. Any document with an accompanying photograph would lend further credence. Any of the above items have shortcomings that make them suspect under some circumstances.

The most common method of identification is by extrapolation. This is also the most common method of mis-identification. This consists mostly of studying the objects, reviewing known written material, and observing related matter. All that is written or observed is not truth; it is, at best, tentative and subject to constant revision. This method involves studying several factors, such as type of material and the glaze. Is it redware (most redware pottery was made before 1900), yellow ware, or hard paste porcelain? There are various glazes, such as lead (very high gloss but generally discontinued about 1930 because it is highly toxic on dining ware), salt, flint enamel (after 1855), or iron oxide.

> EXTRA: Iron oxide or brown glaze is often taken to mean Bennington, but it is also often referred to as Rockingham because it was first produced at Swinton, England, at a private pottery owned by the Marquis of Rockingham.

Ceramics manufacturers are notorious copiers. When one introduces a successful product, others are quick to jump on board. They usually change the design slightly, especially if it is under a design patent. In some cases, though, they try to replicate it exactly. This is especially true of American producers trying to copy more sought-after European products. They also copy designs in other materials, and iron coin bank collectors will be surprised to see several well-known iron coin banks done in ceramics.

Styles, like the famous and much copied hound-handled Bennington pitchers, the much collected Roseville art pottery (no banks), or the Art Deco style which flourished between 1930 and the early 1940s, often provide dating clues. Subjects like the Happy Hooligan, a comic strip that ran from March 26, 1900, to August 14, 1932, can be dated from various written material. All Happy Hooligan ceramic banks likely date from that period.

The type and style of clothing or vehicles also help in identification because the ceramic pieces generally represent contemporary styles. Initially, the slightly stylistic German elephants with comic transfer scenes on them (see #418) were thought to be modern because of the modern tendency to represent older subjects in this manner. However, it turns out all real evidence, such as a 1910 auto and the plain "Germany" marking, indicates they were made about 1910. Having an established date for one piece can then be extrapolated to the next one. For example, another German elephant might have a pastoral scene giving no firm indication of its period, but having established the earlier one with the auto, it can be likewise dated. If an automobile looks like a 1920 or 1935 model or clothes are 1920s, it was probably made about then. If it shows any clue of its contemporariness, that clue should be taken very seriously.

Even color, like the pale bluish green produced by only one German ceramics maker before WWII can offer important clues. That color is found on no other ceramic of any other known period. Once again, having established a date, it can be extrapolated to other pieces with the same or similar characteristics.

An important clue is size. Generally, the smaller the bank the earlier it was made. As money loses value through inflation, it requires a larger receptacle to save a significant amount. Two early pieces shown above, thought to date from around 1870, are so small at 2⅝" they could only hold enough to buy a candy bar today. These pieces are dated by size, clothes, and grooming style — note his lamb chop sideburns and her piled coiffure.

One of the easiest ways of dating foreign-made objects is knowing about the Mckinley Tariff Act passed October 1, 1890, and implemented March 1, 1891, which required the country of origin to be marked on items imported into the United States. These marks are very helpful in dating and determining origins of many ceramic pieces. However, in the first thirty years of the act the country mark was often omitted.

The best example of this is the comic character Happy Hooligan (see *Antique Toy World*, February 1991) who was born March 26, 1900, and died August 14, 1932. Since the Happy Hooligan character was known only in the United States and, perhaps Canada, it is reasonable that nearly all effigy banks were sold here. A number of effigies of Happy Hooligan were produced by the Four Color Pottery Company (FCP) of Austria-Czechoslovakia between 1900 and 1919, a period during which all foreign-made products should have shown the country of origin. Fully half of the Austrian-made products, which were made before WWI, are not properly marked — including Happy Hooligan, a remarkable amount of laxity. If indicative of other products, their lack of country of origin does not automatically mean they were made before 1891. Where there is no country of origin shown and it is an old piece, it could have been made before 1891. But, with the Happy Hooligan, knowing his date of creation (1900) and demise (1932) and the fact that the FCP closed at WWI, by extrapolation it could not have been made before March 1900 or after 1919.

A responsible antique dealer says ceramics marked "Germany" were pre-WWI and those marked "Made in Germany" were made between WWI and WWII. Examination of German-made ceramics tends to confirm this. It is more likely the division was from 1891 to 1921 (when the McKinley Tariff Act was strengthened), and then from 1921 to the outbreak of WWII. In any event, those marked "Germany" are suspected as being earlier than those marked "Made in Germany."

Many early ceramic pieces have "Austria" stamped or incised on the bottom together with control or pattern numbers, usually four digits, but a few early ones have only three. These are similar enough to deduce their origins are the same as those stamped "Austria." In WWI the Austro-Hungarian Empire was a defeated belligerent and the Treaty of Versailles and other treaties dissolved this empire creating new geographic and political entities. Thus was created Czechoslovakia, a country that did not exist until then. Post-WWI Czechoslovakia consisted of three regions: Bohemia, Moravia, and Slovakia. Before WWI these were regions in the Austro-Hungarian Empire. Most of the ceramics marked "Austria" were made in the Bohemia region and we may therefore read most of these marked pieces as being made in what was Czechoslovakia between 1919 and 1992. In addition, there are many post-WWI pieces marked "Czechoslovakia" which were made through the outbreak of WWII.

From March 1, 1891, until September 1921, Japan marked their US exports "Nippon." In September 1921 (when the McKinley Act was strengthened), they were forced to abandon "Nippon" and after that products were marked "Japan" or "Made In Japan." After WWII they were required to mark them "Made In Occupied Japan" until 1952. Only one bank, a wooden puzzle bank, is known to be marked "Nippon." After 1952 Japan returned to marking their products "Made in Japan" and some other clue as to a bank's general period is needed for accurate dating.

Beware of banks with large stopper hole traps in the bottom. They are believed to have become popular in the mid-1960s. These holes allow reuse of the ceramic bank without damage or destruction. The coin traps are both round and oblong. Examination of a few of these traps and trap openings should be sufficient for identification. However, a few older banks have such holes. Most of these are believed to be by Roseville and they may have had decorated cardboard covers glued over them or cork stoppers in their holes. The Roseville banks have footed bottoms. Those we have identified are #634 and #688.

One of the most difficult periods to date is the "cute" style that began about the mid 1930s, perhaps arriving with the cute anthropomorphic Disney characters, and continues through today. The wide eyes, exaggerated lashes, hearts, bows, and pinks on ditsy looking animals are difficult to separate from those through the forties and early fifties. Size is one clue as noted above with smaller pieces thought to be from the middle thirties to early forties. Plates #535 and #710 represent the essence of this style. Some go so far as to have the nose and mouth represented by pink hearts.

There are entire books written on methods of identifying and dating ceramic pieces, and each of them requires extensive study. Be alert to the tendency to want to set as early a date as possible for a piece. This leads to some wild assessments that look absurd in the full light of day. An example of this is #112 in Moore's *The Penny Bank Book*. This Uncle Sam bust, which they date 1860, was made in the 1930s through the early 1940s. Verify dates as much as possible, then be realistic with them.

With the march of technology, perhaps it may not be many years before we will have spectrographic, chemical, and/or atomic analysis of the clay and other materials used in ceramic manufacture that will for certain determine when and where a piece was made. Science may also provide a method of attaching a non-removable certification label to the ceramic piece so it does not have to be reassessed each time it changes hands. Until then be armed with knowledge and experience.

Finally, there is no substitute for experience; it is the ultimate skill in the ability to date ceramics accurately. Today there are several knowledgeable ceramic bank collectors who can look at pieces separately and independently come up with the same or nearly the same date. In most cases they say things like, "Made between 1925 and 1940 and probably toward the latter date," or "Made after 1900 and before WWI." The best way to gain experience is to see as many collections of ceramic banks as possible in museums and other public displays and in private collections. The author's collection is open to all members of the Still Bank Collectors Club of America. Observing, handling, asking questions, and reading are the paths to personal expertise. If you enjoy these ceramic jewels as we do, the paths will all be downhill with the wind at your back.

Condition

All collectors are stuck on condition. The terms mint, pristine, all-original, unrepaired, and other such terms represent the goal of most collectors. Unfortunately, few examples of coin banks of any material come in these conditions. Ceramic coin banks suffer the same injuries and geriatric afflictions as other types of coin banks; but because of their tendency to self-destruct when dropped on a hard surface, they tend to be preserved in mint, near mint, or destroyed and lost forever. With ceramic coin banks there are probably more mint and near mint examples than in other materials, probably in the 15% to 25% range. Overglazed ceramic banks are the best preserved. Bisque and overpainted examples get dirty and/or have the overpaint removed.

> EXTRA: Unlike other materials ceramics do not deteriorate with age. A 3,000-year-old jug is essentially preserved as it was made. Glazed pieces, hundreds of years old, after a detergent washing have a just manufactured look. This is a bonus not found in most other materials and presents the dilemma of distinguishing the old from the new.

The process of describing less than mint requires some comments and caveats. Coin banks were generally made to be handled by children, a risky proposition for banks in any material. Ceramic banks, unlike any other coin bank material except glass, were not likely to get off with minor or no damage in the course of their ownership. To survive intact was almost miraculous. In addition, all early ceramic coin banks were made to be broken to remove coins and most probably were. Then, add the fact that a ceramic coin bank was not a highly valued item and general house cleaning or moving would result in many of them being "tossed." Based on several knowledgeable estimates of ceramic coin bank survival, probably less than 5% survived.

Some collectors are absolutely stuck on acquiring only mint condition specimens. We are not. Probably no amount of advice or pleading will change the mint condition mind set. In some instances a marred specimen can have more charm than a perfect one. Each collector must decide where to set his or her quality standard.

We counsel acquiring pieces that ring the individual collector's gong as a first criteria, even if a piece is flawed. Collecting only pristine examples probably means the collector will have an exquisite but smaller collection. To visualize the possibilities, consider an iron, tin, or lead bank collector who collects only banks without a paint nick or a scratch or a rust spot or some other small flaw. There are not many who can maintain such a standard because prices will be high and opportunities few. It will also result in missing much of the charm and excitement of collecting banks or ceramics. The secret, if there is one, is to pay only for the condition you are receiving. A frequently bent rule.

For us, not collecting flawed specimens would mean passing up or disposing of too many interesting and, possibly, unique specimens. A researcher-collector simply cannot afford to miss that unknown piece. In the cases where an unknown specimen is outrageously overpriced, a photograph and description has to suffice. Flawed examples include the woman with duster and dapper gentleman who have had their heads completely knocked off and reglued. This serious flaw does not show in the display case or in photographs and is detectable only under close scrutiny. Not collecting these wonderful examples would cause a lack in our collection and leave them missing as illustrations for this

book. Perhaps they are the sole survivors of a brief and limited manufacture. Thus far they are the only ones seen by us.

The value of damaged ceramics rises in proportion to their rarity and desirability. Anyone who has visited ceramic collections in museums discovers a substantial portion of the collections consist of broken and/or damaged pieces. Often these pieces are unique and not presenting them in damaged condition would mean not presenting them at all. These are usually rare and valuable pieces. On the other hand, serious damage to common pieces results in the loss of nearly all their value. There are numerous types of flaws from poor manufacture to chips and breaks. Each flaw has to be evaluated in an individual light, together with price and collecting interest, then adjusted accordingly. A good rule is buy only if you believe it is scarce, and pay for the pleasure of enjoying it in your collection until the perfect one comes along. You will not then be disappointed when you sell it for a pittance.

EXTRA: Because ceramics shrink during firing and are almost never uniform in thickness, the uneven shrinkage causes a fire crack. A fire crack usually results in discarding the piece today, but early pieces were decorated and sold; often with the crack disguised. A fire crack is wider at its terminus end. Fire cracks and other cracks are sometimes referred to as "age cracks." No amount of aging can cause cracking. Another "age crack" misnomer is when an old fire crack yellows revealing its presence.

The ceramic coin bank was generally a low-cost production item intended to sell for a very modest price to an indiscriminating clientele. Most sold for pennies to children. This was often reflected in their somewhat careless production. It is not uncommon to find a bank with a chip with glaze over it. This means the chip occurred during the biscuit forming and/or firing of the piece. In some

instances the pieces were placed too close together and part of one bank was fused onto another bank and sold with the flaw. In other cases a bank was fused to the kiln and, when broken loose, lost some of its bottom (foot). Comparing various pieces, it is also common to find details obscured or obliterated on some examples. Here we show Uncle Sam heads by the Four Color Pottery, one is chipped in a number of places

while the other has only one chip but details are so obscured there are no stars left on the top hat and few facial features can be discerned.

For us the least offensive defect is the bottom of the bank broken out, provided no cracks extend out to the bottom perimeter of the bank. This flaw has the charm of knowing the bank was used to collect coins and the child who owned it one day received his or her saving reward. Base chips, those that pulled off when removed from the kiln, flaked off when setting the bank down or even dropping it, are also not very offensive. They do not interfere with the main theme of the bank and are easily overlooked. Chips in other places, particularly in projecting areas like hat brims, noses, and ears are offensive, and moderate to substantial value should be deducted. Chips or cracks from the coin slot can range from modest to offensive. They are obviously caused by children (or desperate parents) robbing the banks. Again, depending on size, location, and effect, each flaw has to be evaluated individually.

Breaks are the most offensive damage and they are sometimes difficult to detect. A piece broken out and reglued can never hold the value of an undamaged piece. Only unique examples retain significant value.

The glaze on banks is frequently crazed or covered with fine cracks through the glaze, this is called a crackle finish. This must not extend into the ceramic; if it does, it is cracking. The crackle finish is intentionally created by the disparity in the heating and cooling temperatures of the ceramic and the glaze. Crackle finish is often seen in Staffordshire dog heads and cabbage decorated cottages. In other cases, tapping the ceramic with a hard object, like attempting to remove coins with a knife, can craze the surrounding area. These glaze breaks have somewhat less effect and should be depreciated accordingly.

There is often a choice between a "Perfect" or unchipped specimen and a chipped one with more desirable features. Consider the two hexagonal bank buildings shown below, the one on the left has the darker roof line color extending down midway into the upper floor windows but has no chips, the one on the right has the roof line exactly where it should be but has chips off the back of chimney and the rear base. Our choice was to sell the former and keep the latter because the roof painting is correct along the roof line and additionally the glaze is better applied and more uniform. These types of decisions are constantly necessary as multiple examples pass through the collector's hands.

All banks should be inspected under magnification for flaws. Another technique is to run the finger over all the edges. The finger will detect a rough-flawed area better than the eye. In most cases once a ceramic bank is purchased, it is purchased. The seller, even if he or she knows of a flaw, will contend it occurred after you bought it and it left his or hands. Buy with caution.

Some banks are colored and decorated with an overpaint. After the piece is glazed and fired, a worker paints on top of the glaze. Two examples are #42 and #43. Usually, but not always, the piece is then refired at a lower temperature to set the paint. Overpaint scratches and flakes much easier than underglaze painting, even washing will remove some or all of the overpaint. Another variation is painting a bisque (unglazed) piece such as #87 (note washed out hat band) and #262 (note grimy appearance). Washing is particularly damaging to bisque pieces. Bisque pieces also tend to permanently acquire dirt. It is often difficult to find satisfactory examples of this type of ceramic bank.

Repairs and restorations are useful for rare and valuable pieces. The cost is usually high and the results mixed. Generally, it costs more to have a piece repaired and/or restored than it adds to its value. We have had a few done to enhance the pleasure in owning and viewing the bank. High-priced banks should be carefully inspected for repairs and restorations.

> EXTRA: Occasionally a glazed bank is purchased that has dirt caked on it. Provided it is not bisque or overpainted, it can be cleaned easily by soaking and washing in regular dish washing detergent. An old toothbrush can be used to clean crevices and hard to reach places. In many instances the seller of the dirty item is not aware it can be easily cleaned and sells it at a bargain basement price.

One easy and inexpensive way to enhance the appearance of a chip or a flaw is to color in the offending area with matched color. A white chip area on a cobalt blue glaze shows badly. A large set of colored felt tip pens can be purchased at any large stationery supply. They can be used to fill in the white area with matched color and it becomes nearly invisible. Before proceeding on an obvious and important spot, test the color match on the bottom, rear, or less conspicuous place. This coloring should never be done to deceive and when the piece is removed from the collection and disposed of, the flaw should be noted.

Prices

Some collectors will want to read the price section first, expecting profound knowledge, expert experience, and a crystal clear guide. If such exists, please send it to us.

Price is a many faceted subject in a constant whirlwind of change compounded by personal inclinations and market flux. Each price factor must be evaluated at the time of a transaction to determine current price.

All serious collectors know rarity is an important function of price. The rarity evaluation, as previously noted, is the best available at this writing. Because this is the first attempt at rarity ratings, they are also in a state of uncertainty and revision even as they are discussed here.

Desirability or charisma is the one big complicating factor in most pricing. Even this factor is divided into two facets, general or public desirability and personal desirability.

Each of these factors can have a prodigious effect on price.

General desirability is nothing more than a bunch of people wanting or not wanting a specific specimen from a limited supply. If out of 200 collectors 50 agree they desire the 20 known pieces, they will drive the price up. If out of 200 collectors 10 agree they desire the 20 known pieces, they will probably get them pretty cheap. General desire is subject to wild fluctuations based on unknown and unpredictable future events. Examples affecting prices are someone brings out a book on a heretofore unknown or obscure subject, an excellent article or series is written, a lecturer preaches a particular gospel, a dealer advertises extensively, or a style, like Art Nouveau, catches the public's fancy.

Similarly, as styles fade, debunking articles are written (the exposé of coin banks from the Bennington potteries, *The Penny Post* 1991 Volumes 2 & 3), books go out of print, demand weakens, and prices slide. To determine current general desirability and to get a feel for an unfamiliar market, particularly for rookies, it is wise to develop a few knowledgeable contacts. Those generous enough to share their knowledge and insights should be rewarded from time to time with a humorous book, an unusual calendar, a souvenir, a thank you card, a box of candy, or some other thoughtful remembrance.

Personal charisma is so individual only the collector-buyer can really assess its impact. We have overpaid for fifty or more pieces in our collection and we have to conclude, "If you love it, go for it." As the collector's eye and sophistication are developed, the desire becomes more reliable. One factor we assess is the "appreciation equation." When the piece is displayed in our collection and we pass it every day, we have a chance to admire and appreciate it. This may be worth $0.10 a day, $3.00 a month, or $35.00 year. Thus, acquiring it now and appreciating it, rather than waiting and perhaps missing a year or more of enjoyment, is worth a few bucks. For pieces that don't stir your personal charisma, we say, be patient.

Cross collecting and its effect on prices is a major factor and is in a constant state of flux. Majolica collectors could care less if a rare and beautiful bust bank had a slot or not. They want it because it is a wonderful example of their collecting specialty, and they bid on it in accordance with the majolica market. Even this can be complicated by a few majolica pieces of comic characters like The Katzenjammer Kids, because comics collectors would also bid to have the boys in their collections. Similarly, with Roseville, Staffordshire, Shawnee, or any of the other widely collected manufacturers, prices will be influenced by collectors of these manufacturers.

There are a few artists who made coin banks. Principal among them is George Ohr, who is discussed elsewhere. He is widely known by ceramics collectors but virtually unknown and unappreciated by bank collectors. They are, therefore, unwilling to pay the several hundred dollars asked for each of his works. Ceramic bank prices are more widely influenced by cross collecting than prices on other types of banks; in some cases, they are ruled almost exclusively by cross collectors.

One recent example of cross collector interest and its effect on values was the Seaman's Bank auction, held by the FDIC in March 1991 by Christie's. American redware banks fetched astonishing prices based on the expert estimates. We are not experts in this area even though we have a few such pieces in our collection. We have relied on the expertise of Lester Breininger who has furnished the information under the USA section and Sidney Gecker who has furnished photos, prices, and descriptions as noted in the photo section. The Christie auction estimates, shown in parentheses, and prices realized at the Seaman's Bank auction were: item 99 (Est.$200–300) $3,900; item 101 (Est.$100–200) $1,800; item 147 (Est.$300–450) $3,900; item 148 (Est.$200–300) $2,400; item 152 (Est.$240–380) $7,000; item 283 (Est.$260–320) $3,600; item 340 (Est.$300–400) $7,250. When items routinely fetch 10 to 20 times their expert estimates, there are mysterious and unknown forces at work that we little understand. We suggest extensive study, wide experience, and expert information before plunging into these waters.

At this writing most ceramic coin banks fetch prices from $20 to $800. Anyone reaching beyond that needs more information. Our values, shown at the end of each listed item, are as of the date of publication, and we anticipate, this work will influence prices upward.

General rules for buying and collecting ceramic coin banks: be aware of rarity; be somewhat patient if you know multiple examples exist; know the current market; assess general and personal charisma; develop information contacts; and be aware of cross collecting potential. And buy what you like. GOOD LUCK!

Rarity Ratings

Partly as homage to former coin bank authors and partly to keep a familiar system intact, this book follows the A to F rating system initiated by Hubert Whiting and continued by Andy and Susan Moore and most other bank authors.

Generally, the reader will find grading much higher than those of iron banks. This is due to several factors. One, the cost of producing a ceramic bank was much less than that of an iron bank and therefore there was a natural inclination toward variety. Even the FCP, the biggest ceramic coin bank manufacturer we know of, made a bewildering number of banks with many just being discovered. Two, the ceramic "plant" could be in someone's backyard whereas an iron foundry represented a large investment and a concentration of producers. Where there were ten to fifteen iron producers, there were hundreds to possibly thousands of ceramic producers. Three, the producers were much more localized and limited in output and few of them sought any national distribution, let alone international sales. Four, a number of potters strove toward individual pieces and as we inspect our collection we find a goodly number we believe to be unique. This we find part of the charm of collecting ceramic banks, we never know what will pop up next.

A census of ceramic coin banks is difficult since most bank collections have a limited ceramics representation, usually less than fifty specimens. There are less than a half dozen coin bank collections that have 200 or more ceramic banks.

The startling fact of previewing other collections is how many pieces we have never seen before. Thus, one of the pleasures of ceramic coin bank collecting is visiting other collections with the certain knowledge you will see some wonderful banks not seen before, and visitors to your collection will have the same experience. This is quite different from visiting an iron coin bank collection where the focus is on the relative condition and the rarities.

A census shows few A banks, a good number of B banks, a whopping number of C banks, twice as many D banks as B's, and E banks about equal to B's, and a few F's. These ratings were given by us after review of most of the larger collections in the United States and one in Europe. Where possible we have consulted other collectors to confirm our opinions. We do not consider any of the ratings gospel and very many of them will be changed based on additional input and experience. In general, ceramic banks were made in smaller quantities per design but in far greater varieties.

Ceramic coin bank rarity is greater than cast iron bank rarity. In general cast iron banks have been so widely sought and collected few of them escaped to the rubbish heap. Whereas, ceramics have suffered a less kind fate and many were consigned to the nether regions. We speculate that ceramic coin banks are less than half as plentiful as cast iron and hope we are incorrect since it will mean more opportunities to add to our collection.

There are other collectors who have collected ceramic coin banks in odd and unusual categories with different goals in mind. Some of our best finds have come from ceramic animal collectors, or people who collect only dogs, pigs, or rabbits, or collect all Japanese animals, or all blue animals. Other cross collecting specialties include majolica, sports, Staffordshire, world's fairs, George Ohr, Roseville, and figurals. At this point, there are probably more ceramic coin banks in the hands of non-coin bank collectors than in the hands of coin bank collectors. This book is intended to stimulate the further interest of coin bank collectors — and of other collecting specialties — in ceramic coin banks.

Unlike most manufactured products, there is a substantial number of ceramic banks that are wholly or partly unique. That is, they are one of kind in some way. Most will fall into certain types and periods, and some will be borderline examples. To be specific, a number of potteries made banks that could be ordered with someone's name and/or a date on it. A number of English pieces, #841, #842, and #844, show individual names and/or dates. They are from 1850 to 1912, and thus were made for a period in excess of 50 years. While they are scarce as a group, justifying at least a C rating, they are upgraded one grade to a D because of their unique date or name or both. Others, like the flower decorated jugs, plates #822, #826, and #829, also have a uniqueness and an obvious pattern. How unique and how individual the flower

paintings are has not yet been fully determined. For the moment, they are considered borderline unique and may or may not justify an increased grade of rarity.

On the other hand, there are those individually made pieces that are one of a kind in terms of style and design, such as plates #1, #593, #670, and #862. If it later turns out there are others, the level of uniqueness can be revised. Art potters generally produce individual pieces, which while they follow a general pattern, have unique and individual characteristics. Since most art potters never made a coin bank, any discussion of their relative merits is irrelevant. The one big exception is George E. Ohr, The Mad Potter of Biloxi, who was a prolific coin bank maker and who proclaimed, "No two souvenirs, on earth alike!" While some of Ohr's banks are similar, no two are enough alike to be called duplicates. All Ohr banks are rated E or F based on uniqueness and desirability.

The rating designations and their definitions

A — Common. Easy to find and most collectors will have a specimen. A thousand or more extant. A small group of A's.

B — Fairly common. Somewhat harder to find. All serious collectors will have one. Less than 1,000 extant. Many more B's than A's.

C — Uncommon. Seen occasionally. Commands higher price. A wait of a year or more may be needed to find a particular one. Less than 400 are known. The C rating also acts as an uncertain catchall between B and D where more precision is not now possible. Some C's could decrease to B and some increase to D. A humongous number of banks are rated C and lower prices generally reflect the large numbers.

D — Scarce. Seen infrequently. Prices rise dramatically as too many bidders chase too few specimens. Less than 100 known. There are a large number of D rated banks, twice as many as B rated.

E — Rare. Usually seen only in major collections of long-time collectors. Less than 15 known examples. Whole collections are purchased to acquire a few of these. The rarest mold made or production banks are rated E, even if there is only one example known, since others may turn up and this is a relatively new collecting specialty. There are about as many E rated banks as B rated ones.

F — Unique or Very Rare. Chances to purchase occur very rarely. A single specimen usually a presentation piece or made for a specific individual such as item 838. Other F banks would be single specimens of hand-crafted banks such as those mentioned above. Similar ones, though unlikely, could turn up, and if several do the rating should be changed.

While most collectors will be satisfied with a single color of a particular specimen, there are those who, like ourselves, will collect every color we can find. Color can easily add a grade of rarity to a particular specimen and in a few cases two grades. We have made little attempt to give color variation ratings and at this writing they have only a modest effect on prices.

Charisma is the wild card in collecting and it does not affect rarity, but it drastically affects price. For example, the small Staffordshire human and animal heads from the late 1800s are widely sought and bring prices substantially in excess of their rarity. They are rated from B to D and are also avidly sought by Staffordshire collectors, driving their prices up. Each collector must decide what has and hasn't charisma for him or her. But when collectors agree a piece is charismatic, prices will exceed the price based on rarity. A favorite of ours is the lion, #696, in the Art Deco style which has a barrel body and a bamboo tail, but which may not appeal to other collectors.

Ceramic coin banks are the greatest unexplored area of coin bank collecting. It has already been determined there are more different pre-WWII ceramic coin banks than in any other material; there are at least 2,000 specimens and possibly as many as 3,000. To this number can be added a substantial number of size and color variations. To get some idea of the unexplored territory, Hubert Whiting shows 13 pre-WWII cast iron pigs, the Longs shows 16, and the Moores 17, a total of 21 or 22 different iron specimens. We already know there are 150 different pre-WWII ceramic pig banks and expect this to expand to at least 250. As a general rule there are many more scarce and rare ceramic coin banks than there are in other materials, and the prices do not rise as dramatically as they do for banks in other materials.

> EXTRA: For reasons that will probably never be known, the comic character Happy Hooligan (or Gloomy Gus), popular from birth in 1900 to demise in 1932, appears as a still bank in only one medium, ceramic. There are no known banks depicting him in iron, lead, white metal, tin, wood, glass, or any other material. There are at least eight ceramic versions, with several color and size variations. Go figure!

Geographical Ceramic Manufacturing Centers

Ceramics manufacturing tends to center in areas where necessary raw materials are plentiful and cheap. They are also best located close enough to population centers so that transportation costs do not unreasonably escalate prices, especially for low priced utilitarian ware. As these areas develop and more expensive products are made, location becomes less important, but skilled labor and tradition tends to keep them there. The Staffordshire area in England is an archetypical example. The Zanesville, Ohio, and Trenton, New Jersey, areas are also well known ceramics locations. Most ceramics in this book come from Europe, the United States, and Asia (mostly Japan). A few items come from Central America and Mexico.

Only a few ceramics manufacturing companies made coin banks. They were a specialty line where distribution processes generally required that a broad line of products be offered retailers. The list of pre-WWII non-bank manufacturers is long and illustrious and includes Wedgwood, Fenton or Norton (Bennington), Lenox, Rookwood, and American Art China Works. Thus, the more we can identify a style, like the mottled spatter-type decoration on the Roseville banks, the more we can connect them together.

Most ceramic coin banks were made in or for countries where thrift and savings are taught as important virtues. These countries include the US, Canada, The United Kingdom, some Scandinavian countries, Germany, and Japan. Interestingly these are also the very same countries where most coin bank collectors live today.

The Americas

United States

Prior to 1900 there were thousands of anonymous potteries in the Eastern United States making a wide variety of products. Only a few of these products can be identified and only a few of them became famous enough to be recognized. Since there was no legal requirement and little commercial incentive for United States manufacturers to mark their wares, few did. The Norton Pottery of Bennington, Vermont, was an exception (no Norton marked coin bank is known to exist). Another reason American manufacturers did not identify their products was some of them produced copies of European pieces. In the early days, European pieces were generally more prized by American customers, and American makers hoped that by omitting pottery marks their products would be accepted as European. Potters also did not mark small, cheap, and insignificant pieces, like coin banks. Thus, nearly all American ceramic products will remain anonymous. George Ohr, being a notable exception, always marked his wares.

Because of the McKinley Tariff Act of 1890, all foreign products, including banks, made after that date were supposed to be marked with their country of origin. It, therefore, follows that those products made since 1890 and not marked by a country of origin are American-made products. This, unfortunately, is not the case. There are numerous reasons why a product was not marked as a foreign product. Some country of origin marks would wash off, especially on bisque pieces. Others could be broken out of the bottom when the contents of the bank were raided. As noted elsewhere, the law was not carefully enforced until 1921 and it is probable some items slipped by after that. Many were brought or shipped back to the United States privately by collectors or dealers over the past century and would not have the country of origin marked on them. Thus, the absence of a country of origin on a coin bank is only a modest indicator it may be American. From those we can identify we know an overwhelming percentage were pottery.

As we know with many of our banks, the country of origin is often arrived at by extrapolation. For example, the familiar Czechoslovakian majolica heads are usually properly marked. But those banks not marked or those whose mark has been removed are still from Czechoslovakia. Similarly, other specimens such as Staffordshire, German numbered pieces, Austrian (pre-WWI Czech) pottery pieces, or Japanese Oriental-eyed pigs are all still from the appropriate places and are obviously not American.

The origin of an unmarked ceramic should first be considered based on careful examination of its characteristics and, if indicated, identified as from one of the known places of origin. After this, it should be considered as possibly American made. If American made seems unlikely, it should be left as an unknown. As the reader can see, we tread here in very muddy water, unlikely to clarify.

Bangorware (Made in Brewer, Maine)

Two jug banks identified as Bangorware banks have the slot rising horizontally toward the stopper on an arc but are not shown. It is only interesting to know there was an active pottery here. An antique dealer near Canaan, Maine, said the glazed Bangorware jugs were made from about 1850 to about 1900; before that the jugs were unglazed. She also

noted the pottery was actually located in Brewer, Maine, but they used Bangor as a location because it was better known.

Bennington, Vermont — Coin Banks from the Bennington Potteries

There are no Benningtons. There are only ceramics made at potteries located in Bennington, Vermont. The two famous potteries are one associated with Christopher Webber Fenton and one owned by several generations of the Norton family; here referred to respectively as Fenton's and Norton's. There is only one authenticated Norton coin bank, known as the Eddie Norton bank. It is an individually made presentation piece made about 1875 for the grandson of the founder of the Norton Pottery with his name inscribed on it. The piece now resides in the Bennington Museum. There are two possible Fenton banks, a toby jug and a Swiss lady. Both are probably experimental pieces made from regular production pieces and are also located in museums. There was no regular production known of coin banks at either pottery. The fame and desirability of Norton and Fenton products are such that many products ascribed to them were not produced by them, including most coin banks.

Old Sturbridge Village

This project is a contemporary replication of an 1820 New England village and farm community located at Sturbridge, Massachusetts. It includes the relocated and restored pottery of Hervey Brooks, who had a 72 year potting career beginning in 1795 and opening his own pottery in 1811. Reproductions of early pottery, including coin banks, are made at Old Sturbridge Village. They carefully incise "OSV" to indicate they are contemporary. There is another such project with a pottery in New Jersey or North Carolina doing similar work.

McCoy (Brush-McCoy)

This company started in business in 1899 in Roseville, Ohio, where it remains operating today. In the late twenties they began coin bank production with sponge decorated pigs, #506 and #508. These banks often carry the USA mark on the belly near the back legs. This coin bank production continued into the forties with over-glaze painted pigs, #526. All these pigs are among the most common of ceramic banks. The over-glaze painted ones are more difficult to get with excellent paint. McCoy's best known products (sailor with duffel bag, professor & tower) are from the forties and fifties, all of which have a characteristic steel twist latch trap and cork covered bottoms.

Roseville

Roseville started in Roseville, Ohio, in 1885, and closed in 1954. After 1910 all products were made in Zanesville, Ohio. They were prolific makers of coin banks, all of which are unmarked. Their earliest banks were apples and oranges (possibly pears) identified in an 1898 Roseville advertisement seeking canvassers. These banks were followed by animals, beehives, and Uncle Sam heads, shown as #39, #273, and #614, in the early 1900s. Most of these are shown in the Huxford's books, *Collector's Encyclopedia Of Roseville Pottery*, Volumes 1 & 2. The sharp snouted sponge decorated pigs, #503 and #505, are Roseville products. There are additional Roseville banks such as the monkeys and frogs. These banks are among the best researched and documented of all American made banks.

Shawnee Pottery Company

The company was founded in 1937 and made a wide line of products sold in dime and department stores. They were one of the first companies to introduce cute anthropomorphic animals with long eyelashes and big round eyes, festooned with aprons and ribbons. None of their products are marked. A few may be pre-WWII, but most are later.

Weller Pottery

This pottery started in 1873 by Sam Weller, who began making flower pots. It closed in 1948 after a long and illustrious history including production of many art pottery lines which command very high prices. In their L'Art Nouveau line introduced in 1906, an 8" ear of corn bank was included. In *Official Pottery and Porcelain* it says the ear of corn is unmarked, but such a piece marked "Weller" resides in a private collection. It is the only known marked coin bank from this prolific company.

Herr Pottery

Elizabeth D. Herr operated a pottery at 2047 North 2nd Street in Philadelphia, Pennsylvania, from 1875 to 1897. The pottery made a considerable number of lead glazed, scroddleware, redware ceramic dresser banks, usually with lion feet (see plate #935). We have seen a number of examples for sale, but they are heavy, massive, and usually have drawer knobs, corners, or feet seriously broken. A pristine example is shown and another resides in the Philadelphia Museum of Art.

George Ohr Pottery — George E. Ohr

Pottery and porcelain, like many products, are divided into two broad categories; everyday articles and art articles. Everyday production articles are made and sold for utilitarian purposes. They are usually made without artifice or pretension. The producers of art pieces are consciously attempting to create something beautiful, unique, and enduring. Art ceramics were produced by a large number of artists and companies. Some characteristics of art ceramics are limited production, strong aesthetic appeal, and most often the work is signed or marked. Of interest to the ceramic coin bank collector is that there are practically no art ceramic coin banks. One major exception among American art ceramicists is George Ohr. George Ohr is the single most famous art potter America and, perhaps, the world has produced.

George Ohr is another American original. Aside from his 20" long mustache and his legendary sexual appetites, he was a man possessed with making pottery. He is often referred to as "The Mad Potter of Biloxi." He carried his work to major fairs and expositions where, with his moustache tucked into his shirt or combed into bizarre shapes, he gave pottery making demonstrations.

George Ohr was born July 12, 1857, and began working in pottery around 1879. He retired in 1906 without passing on any of his processes. His skill with pottery was extraordinary and, according to one chronicler, he responded to clay "like a mad duck in water." His use of the potter's wheel is legendary and after removing a piece he would fold, ruffle, bend, twist, flatten, pummel, and mold it into phantasmagoric forms to enchant us. Often he would add sinuous, intricate handles. Most of his work was free-form and some incorporated various representations of parts of human sexual organs.

His banners in front of his tent at the 1895 Atlanta Cotton Exposition offer his self-assessment: "Biloxi Mississippi Art and Novelty Pottery. Geo. E. Ohr has challenged any potter on earth in variety work. Wonderful, puzzling, trick, souvenir — no two souvenirs on earth alike! Greatest art potter on earth." Several other banners restate these claims in bold capital letters for the hard of reading. He fully expected the Smithsonian to purchase his output, build a special museum, and proclaim him the "Greatest Art Potter Who Ever Lived." While the Smithsonian hasn't done its part, Ohr has been fully recognized, and art pottery collectors are now paying enormous prices for his works.

Among the fair trinkets and gimcracks were many coin banks which are considered art works and are highly collectible. Many of them replicate part of human sexual organs such as clitoris, vulva, and penis. One bank represents the entire female sex organ, including the vaginal opening. He also added personal messages on many pieces. As far as is known all of Ohr's work is marked using different marks during different periods. A few of his pieces are shown in #891 through #894.

Pennsylvania Redware Folkart Banks

(Material provided by Lester Breininger, historian and producer of modern reproductions of Pennsylvania German earthenware at the Breininger Pottery. Photographs, prices, and descriptions furnished by Sidney Gecker.)

Pennsylvania German potters have been producing redware since the beginning of the eighteenth century and the process continues today. A substantial part of the pottery produced was strictly utilitarian. It began to be replaced by other types of pottery and stoneware in the late nineteenth century except for flowerpots. No other American region was as diverse in form or decoration.

It is the enhancement of the clay body and the goodly number of multicolored slip decorations and the use of multi-quilled slip cups that set it apart. The palette is mostly limited to yellows, red-browns, green, and black. The white clay imported from New Jersey appears yellow under the red lead glaze. Colored slips were trailed, sponged, splotched, combed, feathered, and marbleized to create various effects. The ultimate decoration was sgraffito where the body of the piece is dipped into the colored slip or has it poured on, then after it is set, a sharp tool is used to scratch away the slip allowing the clay body to show through. Most sgraffito was made from 1775 to 1825 but contemporary production is replicating this process and modern pieces exist.

Pennsylvania redware folkart pottery banks were not an important production item and rarely occur on inventories and production listings. They were probably only produced occasionally as whimsies and given to children of good customers. The banks were treasured and probably had a higher survival rate than other products. Relatively few of them are signed and/or dated.

Glazed banks with slip splotches are known to have been made by Willoughby Smith from 1839 to 1905 (see #820). Some are marked W. Smith Womelsdorf. Others are attributed to him but were produced at the end of his career.

During the 1880s there was a rapid demise of small traditional pot shops. The survivors did so by producing great numbers of flowerpots and adding novelty items like banks and trinket holders. Many of the molded redware fruit banks such as peaches, oranges, and apples, and the bell, jug, bottle, barrels and domed banks come from this era.

The majority of them were painted because it was cheaper than glaze firing.

Mexico

There are a number of Mexican ceramics imported into the United States or brought back to the United States as souvenirs. All known Mexican pieces are low fired, low quality pieces. Some Mexican pieces have a low ribald humor, example #224 is of a man with his trousers lowered having a bowel movement. Most of the low fired Mexican pieces are easily damaged or destroyed.

Canada, Central America, and South America

There are only a few examples even suspected of originating in these areas. Only a few can be conclusively ascribed at this point.

 Europe

Austria (See Czechoslovakia)

Czechoslovakia – Austria

A substantial amount of space in this book is devoted to Czechoslovakia-Austria ceramic banks. A survey of several collections shows fully 20% of all pre-WWII ceramic banks originate from that region. Many early ceramic pieces have "Austria" stamped or incised on the bottom to comply with the McKinley Tariff Act implemented March 1, 1891 (for further details see Identification and Dating).

In WWI the Austro-Hungarian Empire was a defeated belligerent. The Treaty of Versailles and other treaties dissolved this empire and created new geographic and political entities. This realignment created Czechoslovakia, a country that did not exist until then. Czechoslovakia consists of three regions; Bohemia, Moravia, and Slovakia. Before WWI these regions were merely a part of the Austro-Hungarian Empire. Most of the ceramics stamped "Austria" were made in the Bohemia region and we may, therefore, recognize most of these stamped pieces as meaning made in the Bohemia region of modern Czechoslovakia. After WWI those pieces marked "Czechoslovakia" were also made in the Bohemia region of Czechoslovakia.

There are at least three, and possibly four, identified and distinct large makers and exporters (into the United States) of ceramic coin banks prior to WWII. These manufacturers also sold to the rest of the world but marking the country of origin was not required. These major manufacturers are identified by their products which are closely related to each other in each of their respective groups. Since none of the makers have a known name, an identifying name is being given for each distinct group. Hopefully these names will be replaced by the actual names in the future.

The Hole-Eyed Pottery Pig (HEPP) maker is the first and probably the oldest Czechoslovakian-Austrian ceramic coin bank manufacturer, most of which were exported to the United States. Numerous examples of this pig exist and some examples can be seen above. They all have a drip glaze which looks like various colors swirled together; they look similar to old marbles. They are all press mold earthenware or pottery; have holed eyes; round, protruding snouts; short, stubby legs; pointed ears; and are glazed except some of the stomachs and bottoms of the legs are unglazed. They come in three distinct sizes; the small variety are from 2⅛" to 2¾" high and 3⅜" to 4⅜" long which are common. The medium size ones are approximately 3¼" high to 5" long and these are scarce. The largest are about 4" high and about 6" long and are scarce to rare. The general size, size of the eyes, coin slots, and ears all vary. About a quarter to a third are marked "Austria." It is thought these could have originated as early as 1870 and were probably made until WWI. A few of the small ones have been found with C. D. Kenny Co. (an early Ney York grocery chain) just below the colored drip glaze.

There are other pigs similar to the HEPP that are believed to be imitations of the HEPP pigs. They are #510 and #511. These are produced with drain molds and have the typical drain hole in the center bottom. Some of these are spatter ware, #510 and #512, where colored glaze or pigment is flicked at the object leaving a distinct "spatter" pattern. The spatter ware variety are tentatively thought to have been made in the United States.

The next group is the Four Color Pottery (FCP). This pottery probably made banks prior to the 1891 McKinley Act, and, therefore, some of its banks are from a yet undetermined earlier time, probably no earlier than 1870. The four colors are yellow, brown, green, and blue but an odd color surfaces occa-

sionally because of mixture of two or more of the four colors. The majority of the banks have a block lettered "Austria" incise stamped on the bottom of them. Many also have a four digit incised number on the bottom. The FCP made a bewildering variety of banks ranging from pigs to a weeping moon-man. In addition to banks they made small vases, planters, toothpick holders, ashtrays, and other small ceramic pieces.

The FCP has white clay bodies and come glazed in shades of yellow, brown, green, and blue ranging from very light to very dark. For example, some collectors often divide the brown into dark brown and tan, but the variation merely reflects the lack of coloring material in the tan glaze. A survey of several collections reveals the predominate colors are green and brown — approximately 35% each — yellow about 20%, and blue a scarce 5%. Only one FCP bank has been found with Czechoslovakia incised on the bottom, but it is an indication the company survived WWI. If it did, it rapidly changed to majolica and the Czech Majolica Pottery is the probable metamorphosis or successor. The FCP made a number of banks with the C. D. Kenny Co. name on them. This and other similarities indicate they could also be related to the HEPP company.

A small group of banks, #103 to #111, are believed to come from the Bohemia province like FCP banks. Most have hand incised numbers similar to the FCP and the dress appears from Eastern Europe. One is pencil dated 1901 and they are probably produced from 1880 to 1900. They are very attractive because of their life-like expressions, skin color, and polychrome finishes. They are scarce to rare. At present they are considered early FCP's or special production FCP's.

A large group of banks are light tan to dark brown pottery or porcelain. They often have "Austria" on a raised strip on the back or side. The glazes range from a dark, Rockingham-like brown to a very light buff color. Most of them have a flat bottom, and two examples are #144 and #388. A much rarer variety is polychrome, and these are usually larger but identical in detail; see examples #146 and #652. This company is designated as the Austria & Czechoslovakia Porcelain (ACP). A good number of both varieties have Czechoslovakia stamped in ink on the bottom. We conclude the ones with the raised strips with "Austria" on them were made before WWI, usually in pottery, and the remainder between WWI and WWII, usually in porcelain. The "Austrian" ones include most of the polychromia. The earlier "Austrian" ones may be very heavy porcelain and light seldom shines through, except in the very thinnest spots. Some "Czechoslovakia" ones have only a few letters or very blurred letters and fuzzy ink and some have nothing; these marks were presumably removed when washed.

Finally, there are the gorgeous majolica banks (beloved by all ceramic bank collectors) which are designated (MAJ).

Most of them are human heads wearing various hats and include the Katzenjammer Kids, Hans and Fritz. Approximately 40 different MAJ heads have been identified. The MAJ company also made a number of other pieces including dog in red coat (#367) and floral decorated pig (#517). The majolicas have a doughnut circle on the bottom with "Made In Czechoslovakia" in the doughnut. The bottoms are slightly footed, then recede with a 1¼" raised circle in the center with a four-digit incised control number pressed and fired into it. This same number is also usually painted on the lower rear of the piece. Since majolica is the most sophisticated form of pottery, it is possible that HEPP and/or FCP, both pottery makers, is the predecessor company; and after WWI they converted to majolica manufacture. It is generally agreed majolica is much more attractive and salable than the products of HEPP and/or the FCP. There are no known majolica pieces with "Austria" on them, thus all are post WWI.

A few other examples of banks stamped Czechoslovakia do not seem to belong to any of the above companies. Examples are #519 and #878. These pieces have an intriguing uniqueness and are probably from another company or companies in Czechoslovakia.

England (UK)

Staffordshire — The shire or county of Stafford lies on an angle between London and Liverpool; about two-thirds of the way northwest of London, or one-third of the way southeast of Liverpool. Pottery has been made there since the Middle Ages. Until the eighteenth century, products were cheap everyday items like butter-pots, jugs, and mugs made in cloudy, mottled, black and red bodies of local clays and drab colored salt-glazed stoneware. In the early eighteenth century tin mines began to play out and pewter tableware had to be replaced by some other product. Pottery neatly filled the niche and the great innovations in tableware began; much of it originated in Staffordshire. While some of the more famous potteries manufacture porcelain, Staffordshire is primarily known as a pottery producer, and all known coin banks from this region are pottery.

> EXTRA: The pottery-producing area of Staffordshire is also known as "The Potteries" and the "Five Towns." There are actually six towns; the error was caused by an early author, Arnold Bennett, who forgot to include Fenton in his reckoning. In typical English style, they have retained the quaintness of this faux pas. The "Five Towns" are Stoke-upon-Trent, Burslem, Tunstal, Hanley, Longton, and Fenton. In 1910 they were forced by the central government to combine to become Stoke-on-Trent, but even today each of the "Five Towns" retains its former name and any local will direct you to the appropriate town.

The success of The Potteries was greatly assisted by plentiful local supplies of coal and salt in addition to clay. The area was so successful that coal-fired bottle kilns dominated the landscape, and the resulting smoke and soot obscured the sun so badly most inhabitants never saw true daylight. Today The Potteries thrive, employing more than 10,000 workers and artisans. Royal Doulton alone employs 1,800 and Wedgwood employs even more.

Staffordshire is the home of such famous ceramics innovators such as Pratt, John Astbury, Thomas Whieldon, several of the Wood family, Josiah Spode I, William Adams of Tunstall, John Rogers of Longport and, towering above all, Josiah Wedgwood. John Astbury is credited with making the first Staffordshire figures, introducing flint glaze, and blue and white clays from Dorset and Devon.

> EXTRA: Josiah Wedgwood (1730 – 1795) developed cream-colored earthenware (receiving early royal patronage for it); a veined graniteware; a blackware called Egyptian stoneware; and his universally famous jasperware in blue, green, and other colors contrasted with white in cameo-like relief. Wedgwood is also noted for his civic works, exemplary and innovative labor practices, and support of the American Revolution. He came from a potting family and left many potting heirs. Alas, the only Wedgwood money box was made in the 1960s as an anniversary piece.

Staffordshire money boxes come as figures, houses, small human and animal heads, and sitting spaniel figures and heads. The Staffordshire name is somewhat of a misnomer since there were hundreds of anonymous pottery factories in the Staffordshire area, and any one of them could be the producer of one or more of the products we now call "Staffordshire" money boxes. What is known is they were made in potteries located in Staffordshire and are thus named.

There are many modern replicas of the spaniels and other Staffordshire pieces. Some of the replicas are contemporary and others are late nineteenth or early twentieth century reproductions of late seventeenth and eighteenth century pieces; and these are actually antiques by themselves, but are less valuable to the purest collector. Some replicas are particularly difficult to detect because they are often made from the original molds using the identical materials and glazes. There are a few visible differences between them. For example, the gold decoration on the older spaniel heads is not perfectly set and it wears off leaving only broken traces of gold. The gold on the replicas is set using modern chemicals and is usually perfect. The originals have mouths and eyes with a more natural and folk-art look. The crazing (glaze cracking while a piece is cooling) is smaller and finer on older pieces. To determine the originality and date of a piece the most reliable, but not infallible, way is to have a Staffordshire expert examine it.

The best known and most reproduced Staffordshire banks are the spaniels. Large pairs of sitting spaniels are also often seen; none, however, is known as a money box. The spaniel heads shown as #312 and #315 are from the mid to late nineteenth century. Plate #312 has eight whiskers on one side and ten on the other, a good clue to hand painting and folk art authenticity of the piece. The two dogs, one black, the other white, have only a few gold highlights remaining. The mottled tan and greenish-blue head is nearly identical to the others, except it has no decoration.

The next most common variety of money boxes are cottages, houses, and toll houses, which come in a variety of sizes and shapes. Quite a few are decorated with clay shavings (originally shaved from the mold edges), usually called coleslaw. The coleslaw was added in various places on the buildings to imitate hedges, flowers, plants, or thatched roofs; some, however, is purely decorative. Many pastille burners were adapted to money boxes, or vice versa. Bank #739 is a Pratt piece and has a nice folk art disproportion with the two flanking figures higher than the eaves of a two-story building and two smaller heads peering out from the upstairs windows. Pratt is famous for developing several vivid colors, including the cobalt blue and yellow shown here.

Until the nineteenth century, Staffordshire money boxes were salt glazed and after that most were lead glazed. Salt glaze has a subtle grain or orange peel effect and has a low gloss. Liquid lead glaze was a Staffordshire innovation introduced by Enoch Booth about 1750. Lead glaze is glass smooth and has a high gloss. The best known lead glazes are the sparkling majolica pieces.

Plates #44 through #53 are Staffordshire heads. The human heads are Dicken's characters. These are reported as penny pitch carnival prizes from the late nineteenth century. One has a penciled date of 1891 on it; these are usually dated from about 1880 to 1900. Most are under 2" tall, with the taller ones up to 2⅜".

Rockingham — a generic term referring to the most common type of brown-glazed pottery, is usually manganese and ferrous oxide that has been triple glazed and is also called brown china. Rockingham ware is originally from England, actually Swinton, Yorkshire. The name Rockingham also often inappropriately refers to any brown glaze used on pottery. It is usually applied to a light-colored clay body and is sometimes mottled or splotched brown glaze, sometimes of several tones, frequently resembling tortoise shell. Plates #212 and #359 are Rockingham.

The brown glaze is not necessarily a clue to genuine Rockingham. In 1850, within a fifty-mile radius of East Liverpool, Ohio, there were over 50 potteries producing Rockingham ware and any of the thousands of these products could be misidentified as Rockingham. Another dimension of the confusion is the crazed desire to identify products as from the Bennington potteries. Among antique dealers the rule has been, "If it's brown, it's Bennington." The truth is, if it's brown, it's probably Rockingham-type glaze and occasionally a true Rockingham. Coin banks from the Fenton and Norton potteries of Bennington, Vermont, simply do not exist.

Sussex Ware — A type of lead-glazed peasant pottery was made at various potteries at Brede in Sussex shire due south of London. Sussex ware pieces are usually a deep red with slip decoration. They are often elaborately decorated with snails, birds, and other simple figures, sometimes in two or three tiered shapes. They are frequently white slip decorated with the date included. A number of them reside in the Hastings Museum and are dated from 1790 to 1860. The globular type bank from this area dates back to Roman times. The example shown in #723 is decorated with snails and is dated 1863.

France

There are a some known or suspected ceramic banks from France. A few of the known or suspected are #189, #191, #219, and #364. The faience cat, #293, is apparently a souvenir piece with a place written on the head, but it is mostly washed off. Little information can be found about French ceramics.

Germany

A substantial part of all pre-WWII ceramic banks were made in Germany. The major ceramics making area of Germany was Dresden in the Southeast. During WWII, as retribution for Nazi bombing, Dresden was nearly obliterated. Meissen, one of the world's most famous and innovative porcelain makers, was located there. In *Meissen-Porcelain in Color* the author writes, "The literature of German porcelain in general, and of Meissen in particular, is, for the English-speaking collector, remarkably limited." Virtually nothing can be found about German ceramics manufacturers except a few unverified tidbits from antique dealers. Meissen started about 1675 and is the European discoverer of hard paste porcelain and many other important advances in ceramics. Meissen did not, as far as is known, make any coin banks.

Virtually all of the German identified coin banks are porcelain. The Germans were quite fond of pig banks and, in addition to being noted pork eaters, made quite a number of pig coin banks. Their work is of very high quality and extremely creative; some of our most prized works come from there.

Schafer & Vater

Schafer & Vater operated in Volkstadt, Germany, from the last decade of the 1800s until about 1920. They produced novelties such as figural bottles, flasks, and vases marked with an "R" within a star design. They used the odd greenish-blue color that #233 and #556 have. We believe a substantial number of German coin banks came from this company. Their products are high quality with close attention to detail. At least one company made some imitations of their products. These knock offs have strange off key colors and careless quality.

The Netherlands

Delftware — Delftware is a majolica earthenware product made in both Delft, Holland, and England. The latter is referred to as English delftware. Most are familiar with the blue and white delftware, but it can be polychromatic without any white. Delftware usually denotes elaborate decoration. Most delftware is marked and with a key can be dated. Plates #848 and #877 are examples of blue and white delftware.

Switzerland

Only a few Swiss ceramic coin banks have surfaced, two are #287 and #873. They are all pottery. The cow and cat with edelweisses are redware folk art and are called "thume" pieces. No other information is currently available regarding Swiss ceramics.

Asia

Japan

There are several distinct Japanese ceramics producers including two or three with distinct manufacturers' marks. One shows three mountains, the center presumed Mt. Fuji, with "Made In" above the mountains and "Japan" underneath. Over 90% of Japanese ceramics are porcelain and only a few pottery pieces are known. Most Japanese specimens are made from drain molds. We have no "Nippon" marked banks meaning they were made before 1921. All the pre WWII Japanese banks were made between 1921 and 1942 and circa 1930 or 1935 refers to this period.

In Japan most ceramics were made in bisque or bisquet form in one location and then transported to another for decoration and/or glaze. The painting of ceramics was a family enterprise with no member, including the very young, excluded. The fine detail of Noritaki and other world famous brands is produced by older master painters with world-class skills. The rough, seemingly clumsy, painting of coin banks — with colors running over edges, drooping eyes, unpainted spots, uneven colors, misplaced splotches, decorations varying from piece to piece, and a number of other amateurish details — is that of the very young. They started painting as young as two or three years old and developed their skills with the years. There is a certain logic and poetic loop in having the untrained young producing work for the uncritical and naive young purchaser.

There is a large number of Japanese ceramics with raised, grainy slip decorations. This type decoration is often found in the form of dragons on dinnerware, one of which, with cat decoration is known. Antique dealers call these ceramics moriage and Satsuma, but these terms cannot be verified. The latter refers to early seventeenth century immigrant Korean ware rarely seen outside Japan. A number of elephant coin banks have this raised, slip-paint decoration, such as #409.

MANEKI-NEKO BANKS — This often-seen Japanese cat, usually black, white, and red, ceramic bank with right paw raised in greetings is a symbol of good fortune, see #283. The legend began about 1800 when two similar tea shops competed outside the Ekoh-in Temple in Ryogoku. Both shops had beckoning porcelain cat statues, one gold, the other silver. The owner of the golden cat tea house was a wastrel layabout, but the business was kept alive by his charming wife. To pay off her husband's spendthrift debts, the wife borrowed money from a clothing merchant admirer of hers. The lent money did not belong to the clothing merchant, and it brought ruin upon him. Distraught, he prepared to throw himself into the Sumida River. While fortifying himself on the bridge, his vainly loved woman happened along. He told her his plight, and they decided on shinju (double suicide) in order to be lovers in the next world. Their dramatic deaths brought much fame to the tea house of the golden cat and ruin to the competitor. Thus, its symbol of good fortune became a favored image and was then perpetuated. Most Maneki-Neko representations are from the 1970s and 1980s when the symbol became popular but early ones do exist some dating back to the nineteenth century. Once acquired by a Japanese family, the piece is never sold and the older ones we've seen were not for sale. If one is available, expect to pay several hundred dollars for it.

JAPANESE RABBIT BANK — This is one of possibly 12 Japanese banks, one for each sign of the Oriental twelve-year zodiac cycle. The one shown as #471 is made of low-fired unglazed clay. The Japanese, like most Asians, do not consider the actual date of birth important. All of them celebrate their birthdays at New Years and reckon their birth date by the number of New Years, plus one, that have passed. Thus one person could be less than thirteen months and age two, while another could be over twenty-three months and age two. Before WWII when a child was born, a small clay bank representing the zodiacal year of birth was displayed in order that visitors coming to see the new child could drop a coin in the bank. The bank was broken open and the contents used for some important need. The custom was largely confined to the lower classes and was abandoned after WWII. Only the rabbit has shown up so far.

Photo Notes

1. Each piece is numbered with a description of the subject; the material it's made from; estimated date of manufacture; country where made; manufacturer if known; height (H), always in inches to nearest ⅛ inch and always approximate — see note 5 below; rarity rating (A to F); current undamaged price; and after the photo data any factory marks, incidental information or commentary that we believe will be interesting and informative to the reader. All information is on an available basis. Where not available nothing is shown. Some information is succeeded by a (?) to indicate the information is tentative. Heights (H) are for the subject at hand realizing that many manufacturers often had ½ inch variances in the size of individual specimens — see photo of girl's head below. Where "same as #___ except" is used it refers to being made by the same manufacturer and/or contains the same fundamental information.

2. Color is variable depending on the type of photographic equipment, the conditions under which the photographs were shot, the type and quality of the processing and the printing reproduction process. Many manufacturers also varied colors depending on a great variety of factors. The FCP (Four Color Pottery) factory made most pieces from very light to very dark, and occasionally mixed colors to get strange hues. The ACP (Austria Czechoslovakian Porcelain) company produced banks from nearly white to nearly black; our photo of Turk's Head with Bee demonstrates this. Expect only approximate accuracy when comparing actual pieces to the photos.

3. All the coin banks are three dimensional and a photograph is two dimensional. The photograph, unless shot from several vantages, omits much of the detail. It is always a question of whether to omit part of the date, part of the name, split a decorative detail, or shoot the top and lose part of the lower detail. In every case the bottom, which often provides interesting detail and clues of origin, is omitted.

4. The variety of ceramic coin banks is daunting. We offer guests to our home the challenge of naming an animal or subject not represented in our collection. So far only a giraffe has been named and not found on one of our shelves. Many bank subjects were only produced in ceramics.

5. Sizes are shown where they have been measured. Most ceramic banks are 2½" to 5" high, a few are smaller and a few larger. Many photos have a quarter next to them; this is for relative size comparison to assist the reader. The photos were obtained from a number of collectors and substantially exceed our personal collection. The photo data from other collectors often omits some detail, but we felt it was most important to offer a picture of the bank and not get bogged down trying to fill in all the data. In most cases the data will be in line with the other banks in the particular group.

6. In each section we have started with heads, then busts, then half figures, then full figures, and finally those with other objects. This should make locating a particular bank fairly easy.

Plate 1. Salamander nosed man, redware, 1888, US (?), 3⅛"h; coin slot mouth, fern beard, daisy eyes and salamander nose, F; $400.00 – 600.00.

Plate 2. Fritz – Katzenjammer Kid, majolica, ca. 1925, Czech MAJ, 3"h; numbered 8636 (numbers usually appear on rear neck and in center bottom, center bottom is often broken out to retrieve coins); C; $250.00 – 350.00.

Plate 3. Hans – Katzenjammer Kid, same as #2 except 3¼"h; numbered 8632.

Plate 4. Harlequin, same as #2 except 3½"h; numbered 7699; $200.00 – 300.00.

Plate 5. Clown, same as #2 except D; $300.00 – 400.00.

Plate 6. Jester, same as #2.

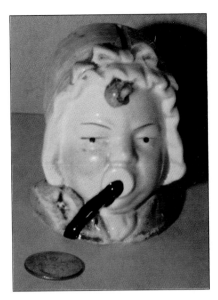

Plate 7. Baby with pacifier, same as #2 except 3½"h; numbered 7697; B; $150.00 – 225.00.

Plate 8. Jowly man, same as #2 except D; $250.00 – 350.00.

Plate 9. Border guard, same as #2 except 3¼"h; numbered 8045.

Plate 10. Boy with stocking cap, same as #2 except 1935, 3½"h; numbered 10186.

Plate 11. Indian princess, same as #2 except 3⅞"h; numbered 7700.

Plate 12. Jockey with cigar, same as #2.

Plate 13. Smoker with beret, same as #2.

Plate 14. Boy with pillow case hat, same as #2.

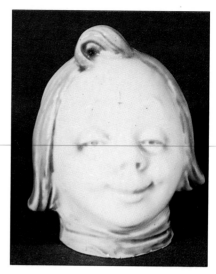

Plate 15. Intellectually challenged boy, same as #2.

Plate 16. Boy with long cap, same as #2 except 3¼"h; numbered 7190.

Plate 17. Girl with tan hat, same as #2 except 3⅝"h.

Plate 18. Girl with purple hat, same as #2 except 3⅛"h; numbered 10187.

Plate 19. Boy with billed cap, same as #2 except 3⅞"h; D; $250.00 – 350.00.

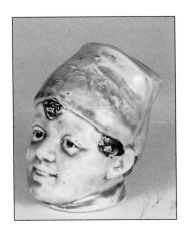

Plate 20. North African, same as #2.

Plate 21. Boy with flowered cap, same as #2.

Plate 22. Boy with cowlick, same as #2.

Plate 23. Crying girl, same as #2 except 3½"h; numbered 9692.

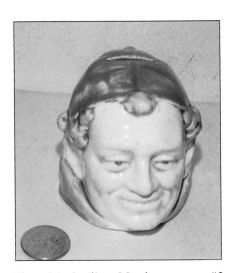

Plate 24. Smiling Monk, same as #2 except 3"h; numbered 7196.

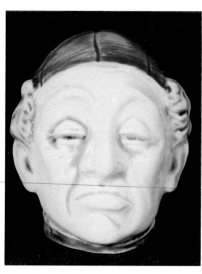

Plate 25. Monk squinting, same as #2 except 3⅛"h; numbered 7195.

Plate 26. Frowning monk, same as #2.

Plate 27. Girl with duster hat, same as #2 except 3⅝"h; numbered 10188(?); B; $200.00 – 300.00.

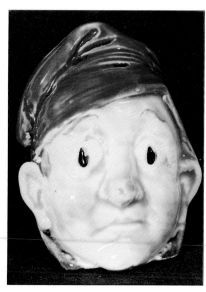

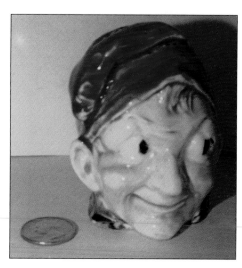

Plate 28. Girl with Egyptian hat, same as #2 except 3⅝"h; numbered 10185.

Plate 29. Frowning boy with red cap, same as #2.

Plate 30. Smiling boy with red cap, same as #2.

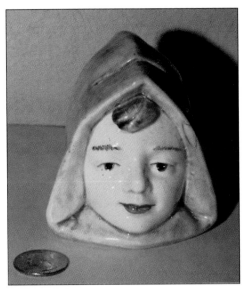

Plate 31. Girl in hood, same as #2 except 3½"h; numbered 10127(?).

Plate 32. Girl in red hood, same as #2.

Plate 33. Boy in brimmed hat, same as #2 except 3¾"h; numbered 10190.

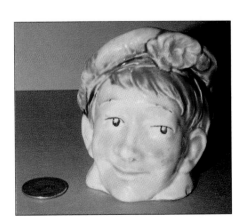

Plate 34. Boy with pink flower, same as #2 except 3⅜"h; numbered 9553.

Plate 35. Girl in Dutch bonnet, same as #2 except 3⅜"h; numbered 7695; B; $200.00 – 275.00.

Plate 36. Girl in Dutch bonnet with fringe, same as #2 except ca. 1935, 3⅜"h; no number, possibly another manufacturer; B; $175.00 – 225.00.

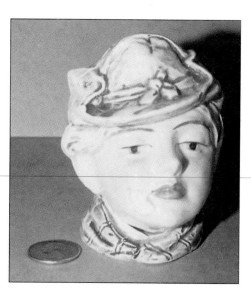

Plate 37. Boy with coat buttoned, same as #2 except D; $275.00 – 350.00.

Plate 38. Boy with flower in lips, same as #2 except 3¾"h; D; $275.00 – 350.00.

Plate 39. Uncle Sam, clay, ca. 1925, US, Roseville Pottery, 4¼"h; gray glaze, known in variety of glazes; B; $175.00 – 250.00.

Plate 40. Uncle Sam, same as #39(?) except unglazed bisque, 4½"h; D; $350.00 – 450.00.

Plate 41. Girl's profile on heart, redware, ca. 1890, US(?); E; $300.00 – 400.00.

Plate 42. Gentleman with lamb-chops, heavy porcelain, ca. 1870, German(?), 2⅝"h; partial overpaint remaining; D; $300.00 – 400.00.

Plate 43. Coiffured lady, same as #42.

Plates 44, 45. 46. Heads 44 – 53 are Dickens characters. Left, Miss Betsey Trotwood, pottery, 1880 – 1900, English, Staffordshire, 2¼"h; B; $175.00 – 250.00. Center, David Copperfield, same as #44 except D; $400.00 – 500.00. Right, Sairey Gamp, same as #44 except C; from *Martin Chuzzlewit*, $275.00 – 350.00.

Plate 47. Samuel Pickwick, same as #44 except D, from *Pickwick Papers*, $400.00 – 500.00.

Plate 48. Joe, Mr. Wardles' servant (blue), same as #44 except C, from *Pickwick Papers*, $275.00 – 350.00.

Plates 49, 50, 51. Left, same as #48 except red color cap. Center, Jarvis Lorry(?), same as #44 except C; from *A Tale of Two Cities*, $275.00 – 350.00. Right, woman with curly hair out of bonnet (unknown character), same as #44 except 2⅛"h; C; $275.00 – 350.00.

Plate 52. Sam Weller(?), Mister Pickwick's servant, same as #44 except 2⅛"h; from *Pickwick Papers*; C; $275.00 – 350.00.

Plate 53. Mrs. Martha Bardell(?), same as #44 except D; from *Pickwick Papers*; $350.00 – 400.00.

Plate 54. Mama Katzenjammer, clay pottery, 1890 – 1917, Austria (Bohemia province of modern Czechoslovakia), FCP, 2¼"h; marked Austria, no control number but many have four digit numbers assumed to be speciman control numbers; C; $175.00 – 225.00.

Plate 55. Hans, Katzenjammer Kid, same as #54 except 2¾"h; D; $250.00 – 350.00.

Plate 56. Mustachioed man with grin, same as #54 except 2¾"h; inscribed (1?)319 (possibly a caricature of Teddy Roosevelt); D; $250.00 – 350.00.

Plate 57. Teardropped head with glasses, same as #54 except 2¾"h; top of curl broken off; D; $250.00 – 350.00.

Plate 58. Teardropped head, same as #54 except 3¼"h; D; $250.00 – 350.00.

Plate 59. Oriental man/Mammy, same as #54 except D; ardently sought ceramic bank, turn upside down to see other head; $300.00 – 400.00.

Plate 60. Chinese bandit, same as #54 except 4"h; C; $175.00 – 225.00.

Plate 61. Keystone cop, same as #54 except 3½"h.

Plate 62. Indian head, same as #54 except 3⅜"h.

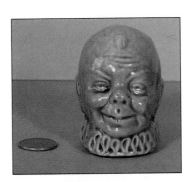

Plate 63. Man with ruffled collar, same as #54 except 3"h.

Plate 64. Pop-eyes, same as #54 except 3½"h; D; $250.00 – 350.00.

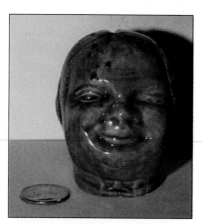

Plage 65. Grinning man, same as #54 except 3⅛"h.

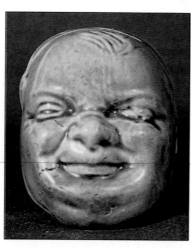

Plate 66. Chubby face, same as #54 except D; $250.00 – 350.00.

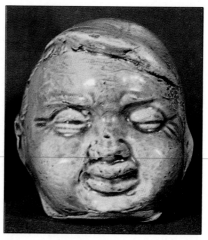

Plate 67. Negro in cap, same as #54 except D; $250.00 – 350.00.

Plage 68. Man with tiny hat, same as #54 except 3½"h.

Plate 69. Thin faced man in hat, same as #54 except 3⅝"h.

Plate 70. Uncle Sam, same as #54 except 4¼"h; note Star of David in hat band; B; $125.00 – 175.00.

Plate 71. Man in hat smoking, same as #54 except 4⅛"h; D; $240.00 – 350.00.

Plate 72. Flat head with coin slot mouth, same as #54 except 2¾"h.

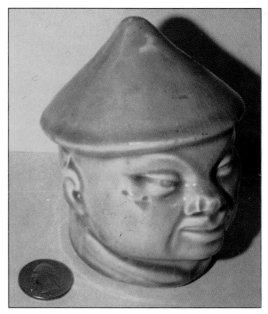

Plate 73. Chinese coolie, same as #54 except 4⅛"h; D; $250.00 – 350.00.

Plate 74. Derby hatted man, same as #54.

Plate 75. Girl with big upper lip, same as #54 except 3⅛"h; D; $250.00 – 350.00.

Plate 76. Bobbed hair head, same as #54.

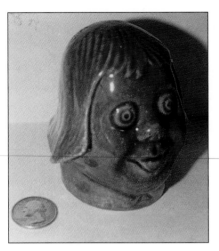

Plate 77. Simpleton, same as #54 except 3½"h.

Plate 78. Girls' and women's heads on box, same as #54.

Plate 79. Smiling girl in Dutch bonnet, same as #54.

Plate 80. Girl in Dutch hat, same as #54 except 3½"h; the only known FCP bank made after WWI, has Czechoslovakia incised identical to Austria; from this we know FCP survived WWI; D; $300.00 – 400.00.

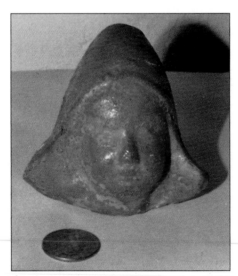

Plate 81. Same as #80 except smaller (3"h) and is stoneware; possibly made using #80 as a pattern, US(?), 3"h; E; $225.00 – 275.00.

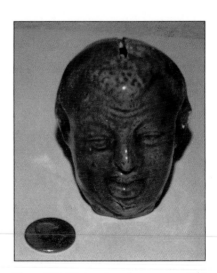

Plate 82. Negro head, same as #54 except 3⅛"h.

Plate 83. Whining child in stocking cap, same as #54 except 2⅝"h; D; $250.00 – 350.00.

Plate 84. Happy Hooligan, same as #54 except 3⅛"h; popular comic character 1896 – 1932; B; $200.00 – 300.00.

Plate 85. Same as #84 except 2½"h; this one is stoneware and may be US(?) using #84 as a pattern; incised on bottom, 260 Feet Mott Well; C; $275.00 – 375.00.

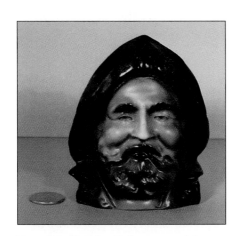

Plate 86. Donitz Ryker, porcelain, ca. 1926, "Made in Germany," 4⅜"h; Ryker was a legendary sailor who began sea rescues; penned on bottom "Mike FROM MOM" 1926; 8021 incised back of neck; C; $200.00 – 300.00.

Plate 87. Black man with bow tie and top hat, porcelain bisque, ca. 1925, German(?), 3⅛"h; 1153 incised back of neck; C; $250.00 – 350.00.

Plate 88. Sailor (possibly Donitz Ryker, see #86) clay pottery, ca. 1925, German(?), 6"h; 2586 incised back of neck; D; $200.00 – 300.00.

Plate 89. Round black man, redware, ca. 1890, US, 2⅝"h; B; $150.00 – 250.00.

Plate 90. Happy Hooligan, heavy pottery, ca. 1910, US, 4⅞"h; HoBo on front collar; other sizes known; B; $125.00 – 175.00.

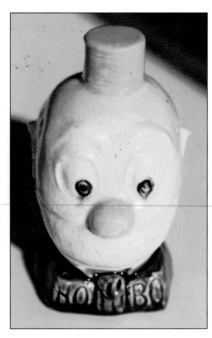

Plate 91. Happy Hooligan, same as #90 except rare color variation; 690 inscribed on bottom; E; $250.00 – 350.00.

Plate 92. Happy Hooligan, heavy pottery, ca. 1920, US, 6"h; "HoBo" on front collar; C; $200.00 – 300.00.

Plate 93. Indian head with headdress and black band, pottery, ca. 1925, Japan(?), 3⅛"h; D; $150.00 – 200.00.

Plate 94. Indian head with blue neck, pottery, ca. 1930, Japan, 4½"h; B; $50.00 – 75.00.

Plate 95. Indian with red, porcelain, ca. 1930, Japan, 3⅞"h; B; $50.00 – 75.00.

Plate 96. Sad Indian, porcelain, ca. 1935, Japan, 4"h; A; $25.00 – 35.00.

Plate 97. Small Indian, same as #96 except 3⅛"h; B; $50.00 – 75.00.

Plate 98. Thin clay Indian, pottery, ca. 1935, Japan, 4¼"h; B; $75.00 – 100.00.

Plate 99. Thin porcelain Indian, porcelain, ca. 1935, Japan, 4⅛"h; B; $50.00 – 75.00.

Plate 100. Thin Indian with rosette headband, same as #99 except 4⅜"h; C; $100.00 – 150.00.

Plate 101. Indian girl, porcelain, ca. 1935, Japan, 3⅜"h; B; $75.00 – 100.00.

Plate 102. Indian with breast plate, same as #101 except 5"h; D; $175.00 – 200.00.

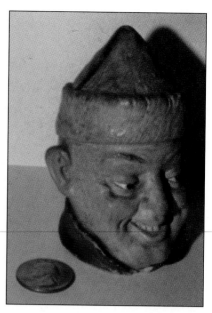

Plate 103. Man in fur hat, heavy pottery, ca. 1890, Czech(?), FCP(?), 3¾"h; 4184 hand incised; E; $300.00 – 400.00.

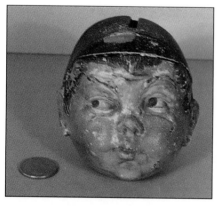

Plate 104. Boy in cap, same as #103 except 3⅜"h, no numbers.

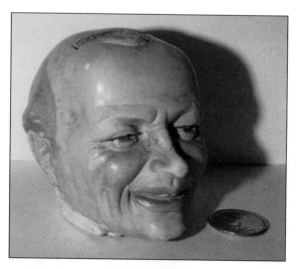

Plate 105. Older man with tuft of hair, same as #103 except 3"h, hand incised 1041; pencil dated 1901.

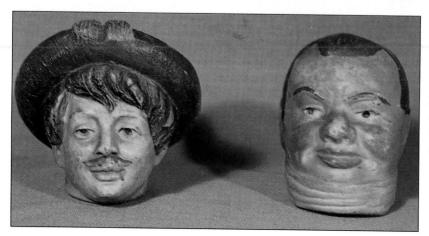

Plates 106, 107. Left, man with tight collar, same as #103 except D; $250.00 – 300.00. Right, Cavalier, same as #103(?) except D; $200.00 – 300.00.

Plate 108. Man in Derby, same as #103 except 4"h.

Plate 109. Monk, same as #103.

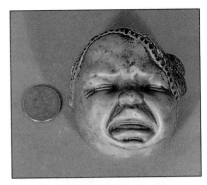

Plate 110. Crying baby, same as #103 except 2⅛"h; 465 stamped on bottom; D; $250.00 – 300.00.

Plate 111. Man with cap and woven straw, same as #103(?); E; $300.00 – 400.00.

Plate 112. Moorish man with turbin, pottery, ca. 1900, English, 4⅝"h; BEST ENGLISH PORCELAIN incised on bottom; E; $300.00 – 400.00.

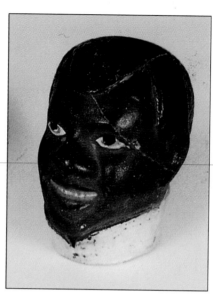

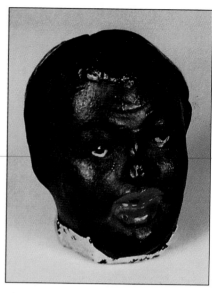

Plate 113. Black man with rag hat, heavy pottery, ca. 1900, English(?), 6¼"h; E; $350.00 – 450.00.

Plate 114. Smiling Negro with white collar, redware, ca. 1910, US(?); D; $250.00 – 350.00.

Plate 115. Quizzical Negro with white collar, pottery, ca. 1900, US(?); D; $250.00 – 350.00.

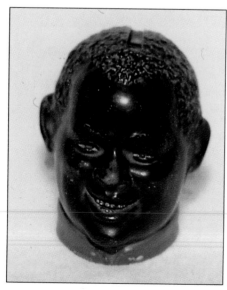

Plate 116. Grinning Negro with red collar, pottery, ca. 1900, US(?); D; $250.00 – 350.00.

Plate 117. Black head and hat, pottery, ca. 1925, Central America(?), 3¼"h; D; $200.00 – 300.00.

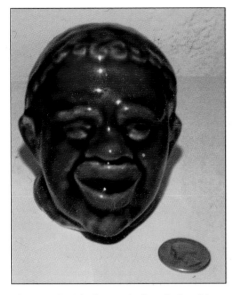

Plate 118. Black man's head, Rockingham pottery, ca. 1900, England, 3½"h; 1816 hand incised on bottom also footed; C; $150.00 – 225.00.

Plate 119. Blackface boy with stocking cap, pottery, ca. 1910, Germany(?), 3¼"h; C; $150.00 – 225.00.

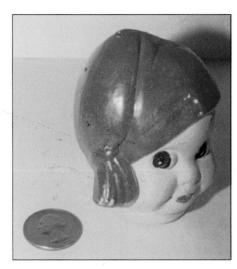

Plate 120. Pinkface boy with stocking cap, pottery, ca. 1910, Germany, 2⅞"h; ink stamped Germany on bottom (similar to #119); C; $150.00 – 225.00.

Plate 121. Mayan man, pottery, ca. 1925(?), Mexico(?), 2⅝"h; D; $200.00 – 250.00.

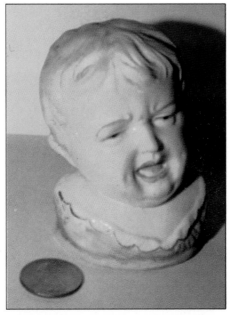

Plate 122. Crying baby, porcelain bisque, ca. 1890, German(?), 3½"h; C; $200.00 – 275.00.

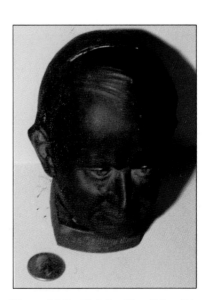

Plate 123. Calvin Coolidge(?), pottery, ca. 1928, American; D; $250.00 – 350.00.

Plate 124. Lovers' heads in dormer window, porcelain, ca. 1880, German, 3⅝"h; 1239 incised lower rear with A underneath; C; $200.00 – 275.00.

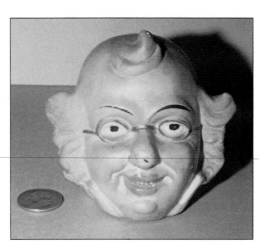

Plate 125. Foxy Grandpa, pottery, ca. 1880, American, 3⅝"h; C; $175.00 – 250.00.

Plate 126. Mr. Slick, porcelain bisque, ca. 1900, German(?), 3⅛"h; 894 incised on back of neck; glazed version known; C; $250.00 – 350.00.

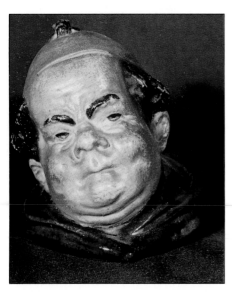

Plate 127. Serious monk, pottery, ca. 1880, Spanish(?); D; $300.00 – 350.00.

Plate 128. Woman in hat, pottery, ca. 1925, European(?); C; $200.00 – 250.00.

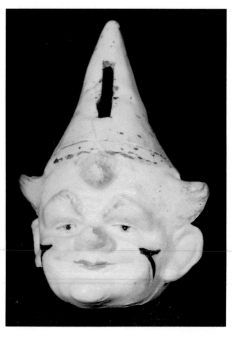

Plate 129. Clown's head, porcelain, ca. 1920, German(?); D; $250.00 – 350.00.

Plate 130. Oriental with drooping mustache, pottery, ca. 1900, US(?), 2⅞"h; C; $175.00 – 250.00.

Plate 131. Grumpy lady, pottery, ca. 1935, US(?), 4¾"h; C; $150.00 – 200.00.

Plate 132. Santa head, pottery, ca. 1948, Occupied Japan, 3¼"h; B; $50.00 – 100.00.

Plate 133. Chinese head, redware, ca. 1910, US(?), 3¼"h; D; $250.00 – 325.00.

Plate 134. Clown with tongue out, porcelain, ca. 1920, German, 2⅝"h; overpainted, mostly worn off; 861 incised back of neck; C; $200.00 – 250.00.

Plate 135. Dunce, pottery, ca. 1900, US(?), 4⅜"h; D; $300.00 – 350.00.

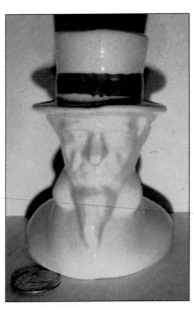

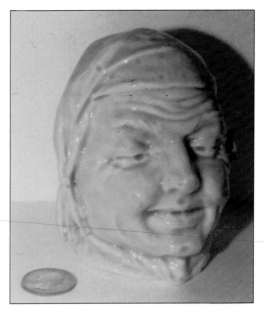

Plate 136. Bearded man, pottery, ca. 1910, Europe (FCP?), 3½"h; C; $225.00 – 300.00.

Plate 137. Uncle Sam, pottery, ca. 1935, US, 4½"h; A; $40.00 – 65.00.

Plate 138. Man in blue nightcap, porcelain, ca. 1920, German, 4⅛"h; slight traces of gold highlights remain; 398 incised on collar; C; $200.00 – 250.00.

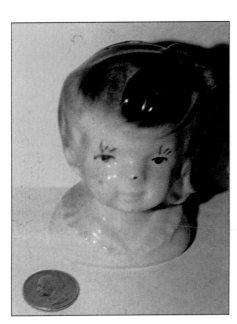

Plate 139. Girl's head, pottery, ca. 1935, US(?), 3⅞"h; C; $100.00 – 125.00.

Plate 140. Grinning man with hat, redware, ca. 1900, Europe(?); D; $200.00 – 300.00.

Plate 141. Prussian guard, majolica, ca. 1910, German(?), 6"h; D; $250.00 – 350.00.

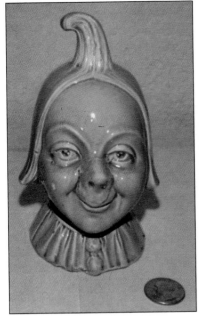

Plate 142. Simpleton, pottery, ca. 1920, German(?), 5¾"h; C; $175.00 – 225.00.

Plate 143. Boy in sailor's(?) cap, pottery, ca. 1900, Europe(?), 3¼"h; D; $200.00 – 300.00.

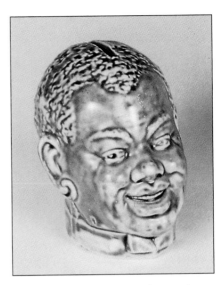

Plate 144. Negro with earrings, porcelain, ca. 1900 – 1930, Bohemia section of modern Czechoslovakia, Austrian and Czechoslovakia Porcelain; this is the usual tan to brown version found early in pottery and later in porcelain; they also made rarer, usually larger, colored premium versions which sell for substantially more on today's market (see #146); C; $150.00 – 200.00.

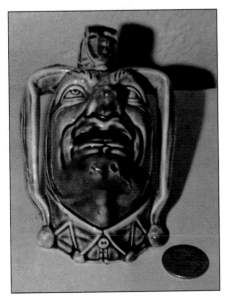

Plate 145. Jester looking up, same as #144 except 3⅝"h; C; $175.00 – 225.00.

Plate 146. Jester looking up, same as #145 except scarce colored version; E; $350.00 – 450.00.

Plate 147. Wind face same as #144.

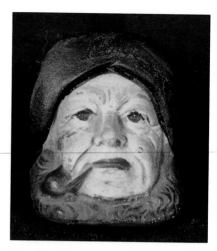

Plate 148. Japanese soldier, same as #144 except 3⅜"h; D; $250.00 – 275.00.

Plate 149. Turk head with bee, same as #144 except 3½"h; C; $150.00 – 190.00.

Plate 150. Donitz Ryker(?), see #86, pottery, ca. 1920, Europe(?); C; $150.00 – 190.00.

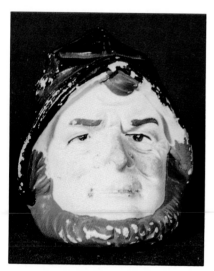

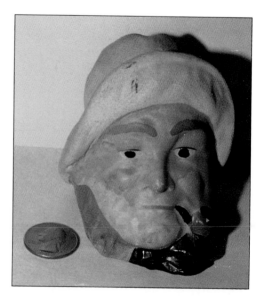

Plate 151. Donitz Ryker(?), see #86; C; $150.00 – 190.00.

Plate 152. Donitz Ryker(?), see #86; C; $150.00 – 190.00.

Plate 153. Donitz Ryker(?), see #86, 3½"h; C; $150.00 – 190.00.

Plate 154. Man in the Moon, same as #54 except D; $275.00 – 350.00.

Plate 155. Shrunken head, pottery, ca. 1890, US(?), 2⅝"h; D; $250.00 – 300.00.

Plate 156. Hairy head, pottery, ca. 1880, US(?); E; $350.00 – 450.00.

Plate 157. Pumpkin head, pottery, ca. 1880, US(?); E; $350.00 – 450.00.

Plate 158. Mischevious boy, pottery, ca. 1925, Europe(?); C; $150.00 – 190.00.

Plate 159. Old clown, pottery, ca. 1900, Europe(?), 4⅜"h; D; $250.00 – 300.00.

Plate 160. Toothless woman, pottery, ca. 1910, English Rockingham, 4⅛"h; footed; B; $125.00 – 165.00.

Plate 161. Bow tied man, pottery, ca. 1915, English Rockingham; B; $125.00 – 175.00.

Plate 162. Bow tied man, similar to #161 except more chest and scarce white color 4⅛"h; footed; D; $225.00 – 275.00.

Plate 163. Stocking capped head, pottery, ca. 1910, English, 3"h; C; $200.00 – 250.00.

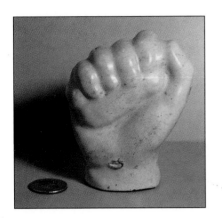

Plate 164. Hand holding clay, salt glazed redware, ca. 1880, US(?), 3⅞"h; F; $400.00 – 500.00.

Plate 165. Chief Red Cloud, Sioux, porcelain, ca. 1925, German, 5½"h; name incised on back with 1136 on lower back and 1142 hand incised on bottom; E; $450.00 – 550.00.

Plate 166. English gent, pottery, ca. 1890, English(?), Rockingham(?), 3⅝"h; B; $125.00 – 165.00.

Plate 167. North African, pottery, ca. 1900, Staffordshire; note mustache, wavey black hair; D; $250.00 – 350.00.

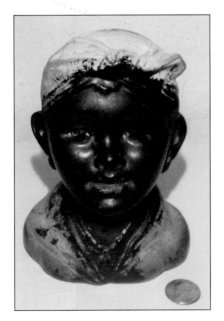

Plate 168. Black boy, pottery, ca. 1900, European, 6¼"h; note all features are Caucasian, may be an art pottery piece; E; $350.00 – 450.00.

Plate 169. Abe Lincoln(?), redware pottery, ca. 1890, US(?), 5¾"h; E; $350.00 – 450.00.

Plate 170. Black sticking tongue out, pottery(?), ca. 1890, Staffordshire(?), 3¾"h; D; $300.00 – 400.00.

Plate 171. Woman with red hair, pottery, ca. 1890, Europe(?), 3⅝"h; D; $200.00 – 300.00.

Plate 172. Woman in duster, porcelain, ca. 1910, German, 3⅝"h; C; $150.00 – 200.00.

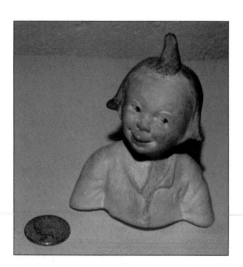

Plate 173. Elf, pottery, ca. 1900, Europe(?), 4"h; F; $350.00 – 450.00.

Plate 174. Man with yarmulka, pottery, ca. 1930, US(?), 4⅛"h; large oblong stopper hole indicates 1960 or later but comes from Corby collection, Corby died 1954; pleasing bank; C; $100.00 – 150.00.

Plate 175. Italian man, majolica, ca. 1930, Europe(?); D; $275.00 – 350.00.

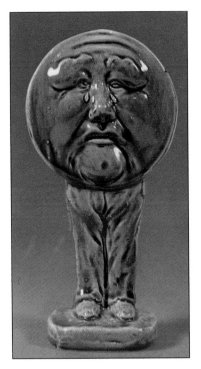

Plate 176. Weeping moonman, same as #54 except D; $225.00 – 275.00.

Plate 177. Sitting eggman, heavy porcelain, ca. 1930, Japan, Acme Ware, 6⅛"h; Acme Ware in wreath on bottom; the only bank we know of designed to sit on shelf edge; B; $100.00 – 125.00.

Plate 178. Eggman with red cap, porcelain, ca. 1930, Japan(?); C; $100.00 – 125.00.

Plate 179. Eggman with green cap, pottery, ca. 1940, US, 3¾"h; B; $100.00 – 125.00.

Plate 180. Mushroom man, pottery, ca. 1920, Europe; C; $200.00 – 250.00.

Plate 181. Middy Bank, pottery, ca. 1900, English(?); D; $225.00 – 275.00.

Plate 182. Man in Derby and top-coat, same as #144 except 3⅞"h; Austria incised on strip on rear coat; B; $100.00 – 145.00.

Plate 183. Man in Derby and topcoat, same as #144 except colored version, 4¾"h (there is a 4"h colored version); E; $350.00 – 400.00.

Plate 184. Happy Hooligan, same as #54 except 5¾"h; 1158 incised on bottom; B; $100.00 – 150.00.

Plate 185. Gloomy Gus, same as #54 except 5½"h; 1157 incised on bottom; C; $175.00 – 225.00.

Plate 186. Prussian Guard, porcelain, ca. 1910, Germany, 4⅝"h; 6664 incised on lower rear; C; $175.00 – 225.00.

Plate 187. German infantry-man, same as #186 except 3⅝"h; 1809 incised on lower rear.

Plate 188. Japanese sailor, same as #101 except 3⅝"h; D; $175.00 – 225.00.

Plate 189. French sailor, pottery, ca. 1900, France(?); D; $225.00 – 275.00.

Plate 190. Girl with basket, pottery, ca. 1910, German, 4⅜"h; Germany incised on bottom; D; $250.00 – 300.00.

Plate 191. Old woman with broom and cat, majolica, ca. 1920, France, 4½"h; 6536 marked underglaze; ink stamped on bottom E/DEVE in rectangle Sarrequem-ines France below; this is only one of a very few marked banks we know of by this well known majolica manufacturer; some suggest the MAJ pieces are made by them; D; $275.00 – 350.00.

Plate 192. Girl in sunsuit with umbrella, same as #101 except 3⅝"h; D; $225.00 – 275.00.

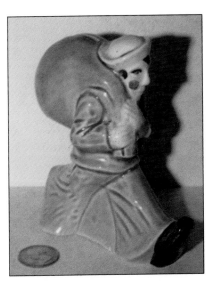

Plate 193. Sailor with duffel bag, same as #101 except 4⅞"h; C; $150.00 – 175.00.

Plate 194. Girl on sled, porcelain, ca. 1925, Germany(?); C; $175.00 – 225.00.

Plate 195. Girl with rolled blanket, same as #54 except 3⅝"h, 1896 incised on bottom.

Plate 196. Woman holding ball, same as #2.

Plate 197. Fat man sleeping, pottery, ca. 1920, Germany(?); C; $175.00 – 200.00.

Plate 198. Man lying on back, pottery, ca. 1920, European(?); D; $225.00 – 250.00.

Plate 199. Dutch Boy, pottery, ca. 1930, Germany; C; $175.00 – 200.00.

Plate 200. Two children, porcelain, ca. 1910, European(?); C; $175.00 – 225.00.

Plate 201. Boy on chamber pot, porcelain, ca. 1920, German(?); C; $175.00 – 225.00.

Plate 202. Black woman eating watermelon, pottery, ca. 1920, US(?), 4½"h; 4089 shown on lower rear; C; $200.00 – 250.00.

Plate 203. Negro girl with basket, same as #54 except 4⅝"h; 2338 incised on bottom; C; $200.00 – 250.00.

Plate 204. Samurai, same as #101 except bisque, 3½"h; C; $125.00 – 150.00.

Plate 205. Diakoku, pottery, ca. 1900, Japan, 5⅝"h; Diakoku is a demi-god patron of merchants; E; $275.00 – 350.00.

Plate 206. Diakoku, same as #205 except ca. 1880, 5"h; E; $300.00 – 400.00.

Plate 207. Diakoku, same as #101 except 3⅛"h; C; $150.00 – 200.00.

Plate 208. Ebisu, god of fishermen, pottery, ca. 1930, Japan, 4¼"h; D; $200.00 – 250.00.

Plate 209. Clown juggler, same as #54 except 5¼"h; scarce blue color; D; $250.00 – 300.00.

Plate 210. Black woman with apron, pottery, ca. 1940, US; B; $100.00 – 125.00.

Plate 211. Man holding money satchel, porcelain, ca. 1925, Europe, 4¼"h; "Time is Money" incised on front of satchel; C; $175.00 – 225.00.

Plate 212. Man holding pitcher, pottery, ca. 1910, English, Rockingham, 4¼"h; B; $100.00 – 130.00.

Plate 213. St. Nicholas with broom, pottery, ca. 1900, European; D; $200.00 – 240.00.

Plate 214. St. Nicholas with long coat, pottery, ca. 1900, European; D; $200.00 – 250.00.

Plate 215. Guessing Bank figure, pottery, ca. 1890, US; same figure on well known mechanical guessing bank Davidson #222; D; $225.00 – 300.00.

Plate 216. John Howard 1726 – 1790 Famed Humanitarian, pottery, ca. 1940 – 50 US, McCoy Pottery, 8¾"h; quoted title on front, back, "The Howard Savings Institution Chartered 1857 New Jersey"; C; $125.00 – 150.00.

Plate 217. Butcher sharpening a knife, porcelain, ca. 1925, German, 3¾"h; 2370 incised on lower rear; C; $175.00 – 200.00.

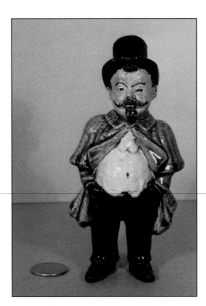

Plate 218. King on throne, pottery, ca. 1930, US(?), 5"h; C; $150.00 – 175.00.

Plate 219. Dapper continental, pottery, ca. 1900, French(?), 5¾"h; D; $225.00 – 275.00.

Plate 220. Man with money bags, porcelain, ca. 1925, German; C; $175.00 – 200.00.

Plate 221. Monk, porcelain, ca. 1920, European; C; $175.00 – 225.00.

Plate 222. Big eyed man, low fired pottery, ca. 1930, Mexican, 6⅝"h; very fragile; note fingers missing from left hand; C; $125.00 – 150.00.

Plate 223. Obese man, low fired pottery, ca. 1930, Mexican; B; $85.00 – 120.00.

Plate 212. Man holding pitcher, pottery, ca. 1910, English, Rockingham, 4¼"h; B; $100.00 – 130.00.

Plate 213. St. Nicholas with broom, pottery, ca. 1900, European; D; $200.00 – 240.00.

Plate 214. St. Nicholas with long coat, pottery, ca. 1900, European; D; $200.00 – 250.00.

Plate 215. Guessing Bank figure, pottery, ca. 1890, US; same figure on well known mechanical guessing bank Davidson #222; D; $225.00 – 300.00.

Plate 216. John Howard 1726 – 1790 Famed Humanitarian, pottery, ca. 1940 – 50 US, McCoy Pottery, 8¾"h; quoted title on front, back, "The Howard Savings Institution Chartered 1857 New Jersey"; C; $125.00 – 150.00.

Plate 217. Butcher sharpening a knife, porcelain, ca. 1925, German, 3¾"h; 2370 incised on lower rear; C; $175.00 – 200.00.

Plate 218. King on throne, pottery, ca. 1930, US(?), 5"h; C; $150.00 – 175.00.

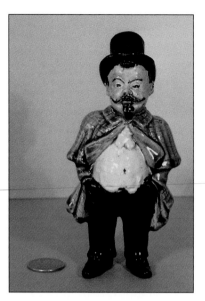

Plate 219. Dapper continental, pottery, ca. 1900, French(?), 5¾"h; D; $225.00 – 275.00.

Plate 220. Man with money bags, porcelain, ca. 1925, German; C; $175.00 – 200.00.

Plate 221. Monk, porcelain, ca. 1920, European; C; $175.00 – 225.00.

Plate 222. Big eyed man, low fired pottery, ca. 1930, Mexican, 6⅝"h; very fragile; note fingers missing from left hand; C; $125.00 – 150.00.

Plate 223. Obese man, low fired pottery, ca. 1930, Mexican; B; $85.00 – 120.00.

Plate 224. Fat man defecating, low fired pottery, ca. 1930, Mexican, 5"h; C; $75.00 – 100.00.

Plate 225. Jack in the box, same as #54 except 4¾"h; A; $75.00 – 125.00.

Plate 226. Happy Hooligan in a barrel, same as #54 except 4⅜"h; 1920 incised on bottom, not a date; B; $125.00 – 165.00.

Plate 227. Happy Hooligan sitting on egg, same as #54.

Plate 228. Keystone cop sitting on egg, same as #54.

Plate 229. Boy sitting on egg, same as #54 except 4¾"h.

Plate 232. Three girls in a bag, same as #54 except D; $225.00 – 275.00.

Plate 230. Girl with cap sitting on egg, same as #54 except 4⅜"h; 1801 incised on bottom.

Plate 231. Santa with "Merry Xmas" bag, same as #54 except 5⅛"h; "1916" incised on bottom; also know with advertising; B; $150.00 – 200.00.

Plate 235. G. Washington(?) on horse, pottery, ca. 1910, US(?), 6⅜"h; C; $175.00 – 225.00.

Plates 233, 234. Left, devil's head on money box, porcelain, ca. 1925, German, Schafer and Vater(?), 4½"h, C; $250.00 – 350.00. Right, devil's head without arm, same as #233 except smaller; D; $300.00 – 400.00.

Plate 236. Boy with spoon riding pig, porcelain, ca. 1910, German; D; $300.00 – 375.00.

Plate 237. Boy with carrot riding pig, same as #233.

Plate 238. Clown emerging from egg, porcelain, ca. 1925, German(?); D; $250.00 – 350.00.

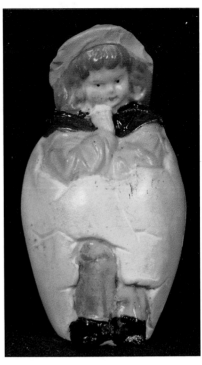

Plate 239. Child in egg, pottery, ca. 1900, European; D; $225.00 – 250.00.

Plate 240. Girl in egg, heavy bisque porcelain, ca. 1870, European, 2⅞"h; C; $200.00 – 225.00.

Plate 241. Girl hiding in basket, pottery, ca. 1890, European, 2⅝"h; C; $200.00 – 225.00.

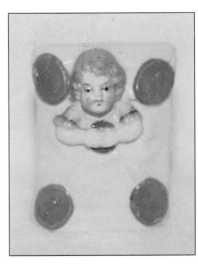

Plate 242. Child in sealed envelope, porcelain, ca. 1910, German(?); D; $250.00 – 300.00.

Plate 243. Cupid with heart, porcelain(?), ca. 1900, European; D; $225.00 – 250.00.

Plate 244. Girl holding plain box, heavy porcelain, ca. 1870, European, 3"h; B; $150.00 – 200.00.

Plate 245. Girl holding red striped box, heavy porcelain, ca. 1885, European, 3"h; C; $200.00 – 250.00.

Plate 246. Girl saving in box between feet, porcelain, ca. 1900, European; D; $300.00 – 350.00.

Plate 247. Woman holding box on lap, porcelain, ca. 1890, English(?); D; $250.00 – 300.00.

Plate 248. Man holding satchel on lap, same as #247.

Plate 249. Boy holding basket on lap, same as #247.

Plate 250. Child putting coin in bank, heavy porcelain, ca. 1900, European(?); C; $200.00 – 275.00.

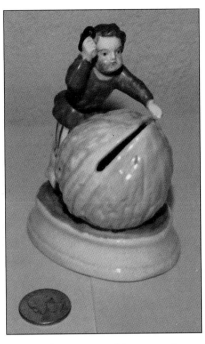

Plate 251. Boy cracking nut, heavy porcelain, ca. 1900, German(?), 4½"h; E; $325.00 – 400.00.

Plate 252. Oriental children, at plum bank, porcelain, ca. 1930, China(?), 3¾"h; popular Chinese symbol but usually not a bank; D; $200.00 – 250.00.

Plate 253. Black boy playing accordian on melon, porcelain bisque, ca. 1925, German(?), 4⅜"h; C; $250.00 – 275.00.

Plate 254. Boy jumping on ball, pottery, ca. 1920, English(?), 4⅞"h; D; $225.00 – 250.00.

Plate 255. Girl jumping on ball, same as #254.

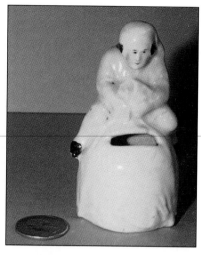

Plate 256. Man on money sack, porcelain, ca. 1900, German(?), 3⅝"h; C; $175.00 – 200.00.

Plate 257. Girl on bed, porcelain, ca. 1910, German, 2½"h; 1557 incised on foot of bed; D; $300.00 – 350.00.

Plate 258. Child and dog on bed, porcelain, ca. 1910, German(?); D; $225.00 – 275.00.

Plate 259. Baby in carriage, porcelain(?), ca. 1930, European(?); D; $200.00 – 250.00.

Plate 260. St. Claus Bank, pottery, ca. 1910, European(?); D; $200.00 – 250.00.

Plate 261. Clown at chimney, porcelain, ca. 1920, German; "Ich Spare" or "I Save" on front; D; $250.00 – 275.00.

Plate 262. Child nursing pig, porcelain bisque, ca. 1920, German(?) 3½"h; D; $275.00 – 350.00.

Plate 263. Black baby in wash tub, pottery, ca. 1930, US(?), 4"h; D; $175.00 – 225.00.

Plate 264. Man sitting at desk, same as #101 except 4⅛"h; C; $150.00 – 175.00.

Plate 265. Comic woman at desk, same as #191 except 5⅝"h; "Droite Besee"(?), "Opera Mundi, Digod"(?) on bottom; slightly footed; D; $175.00 – 200.00.

Plate 266. Papoose, porcelain, ca. 1920, Germany; C; $150.00 – 175.00.

Plate 267. Tommy in a tank, pottery, ca. 1915, English, 3⅞"h; "Where's the blinkin Kaiser?" inscribed on side of tank; B; $150.00 – 175.00.

Plate 268. Mexicans at cactus, same as #101 except 3⅞"h; A; $75.00 – 100.00.

Plate 269. Mexican couple with suitcase, same as #101 except 3⅛"h; B; $100.00 – 125.00.

Plate 270. Elf cutting fruit, porcelain bisque, ca. 1925, German(?), D; $225.00 – 275.00.

Plate 271. Jockey leaning on money bag, porcelain, ca. 1910, German(?), 2¾"h, C; $200.00 – 275.00.

Plate 272. War Monument Viribus Unitis (Stongly United), porcelain, ca. 1910, European, D; $200.00 – 250.00.

Plate 273. Cat's head, pottery, Roseville Pottery, Ohio, US 2¼"h; one of an animal series in this glaze; C; $300.00 – 350.00.

Plate 274. Cat's head with bow, porcelain, ca. 1910, Germany(?), 2½"h; C; $225.00 – 275.00.

Plate 275. Cat's head with heart, same as #54 except 3¼"h; C; $175.00 – 225.00.

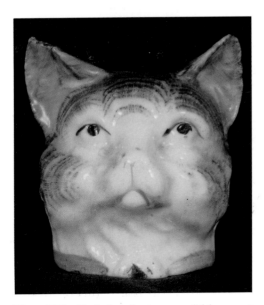

Plate 276. Cat's head, same as #44 except C; $325.00 – 375.00.

Plate 277. Cat's head with yellow eyes, porcelain, ca. 1925, Europe(?); D; $225.00 – 250.00.

Plate 278. Cat's head with bow tie, same as #54 except C; $175.00 – 200.00.

Plate 279. Cat's head, same as #54(?) except D; $200.00 – 250.00.

Plate 280. Cat with coat and hat, same as #54 except 4⅜"h; C; $175.00 – 200.00.

Plate 281. Cat with blanket, same as #144 except 3⅞"h; Austria on raised strip on back; B; $135.00 – 175.00.

Plate 282. Cat with blanket, same as #281, scarce colored version, 4⅞"h; D; $300.00 – 375.00.

Plate 283. Maneki-Neko, pottery, ca. 1930, Japan, 5⅜"h; these early pieces rarely come on the market and are priced very high; D; $350.00 – 450.00.

Plate 284. Black and white cat, porcelain, ca. 1930, Japan, 5"h; bottom has a three peak mountain symbol, probably Mt. Fuji; B; $100.00 – 125.00.

Cats

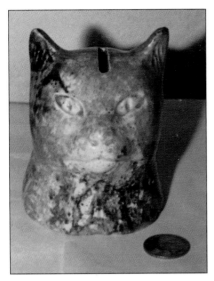

Plate 273. Cat's head, pottery, Roseville Pottery, Ohio, US 2¼"h; one of an animal series in this glaze; C; $300.00 – 350.00.

Plate 274. Cat's head with bow, porcelain, ca. 1910, Germany(?), 2½"h; C; $225.00 – 275.00.

Plate 275. Cat's head with heart, same as #54 except 3¼"h; C; $175.00 – 225.00.

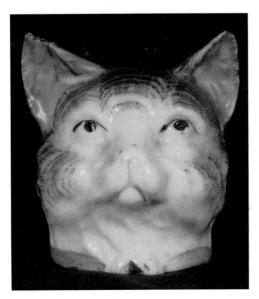

Plate 276. Cat's head, same as #44 except C; $325.00 – 375.00.

Plate 277. Cat's head with yellow eyes, porcelain, ca. 1925, Europe(?); D; $225.00 – 250.00.

Plate 278. Cat's head with bow tie, same as #54 except C; $175.00 – 200.00.

Plate 279. Cat's head, same as #54(?) except D; $200.00 – 250.00.

Plate 280. Cat with coat and hat, same as #54 except 4⅜"h; C; $175.00 – 200.00.

Plate 281. Cat with blanket, same as #144 except 3⅞"h; Austria on raised strip on back; B; $135.00 – 175.00.

Plate 282. Cat with blanket, same as #281, scarce colored version, 4⅞"h; D; $300.00 – 375.00.

Plate 283. Maneki-Neko, pottery, ca. 1930, Japan, 5⅜"h; these early pieces rarely come on the market and are priced very high; D; $350.00 – 450.00.

Plate 284. Black and white cat, porcelain, ca. 1930, Japan, 5"h; bottom has a three peak mountain symbol, probably Mt. Fuji; B; $100.00 – 125.00.

Plate 285. Red cat with bow collar, pottery, ca. 1920, European(?); C; $150.00 – 200.00.

Plate 286. Sitting cat with collar, pottery, ca. 1910, Europe(?), possibly Rockingham, 5"h; D; $250.00 – 300.00.

Plate 287. Flowered cat, redware pottery, ca. 1900, Swiss Thume folkware, 3⅜"h; note edelweiss on rear leg identifying it as Swiss; E; $400.00 – 500.00.

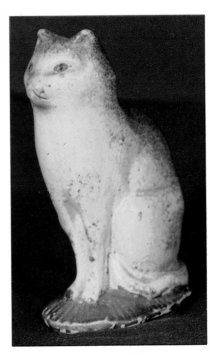

Plate 288. Kitty bank (similar to Moore #343), pottery, ca. 1935, US; B; $90.00 – 120.00.

Plate 289. Kitty bank, pottery, ca. 1940 Rio Hondo Potteries, El Monte, CA, 4⅛"h; B; $90.00 – 110.00.

Plate 290. Slim cat, redware pottery, ca. 1890, US(?); D; $225.00 – 275.00.

Plate 291. Cat on base, pottery, ca. 1900, US(?); D; $225.00 – 275.00.

Plate 292. Snarling cat, pottery, ca. 1935, US(?), 5⅛"h; C; $100.00 – 150.00.

Plate 293. Cat with ball, faience pottery, ca. 1890, French, 2⅝"h; E; $300.00 – 375.00.

Plate 294. Mechanical cat, pottery, ca. 1940, Japan, 5"h; head is on a steel spring, deposit of coin causes head to bob; only one of three similar early ceramic mechanical banks; all have the same body; D; $250.00 – 350.00.

Plate 295. Cat playing string bass, porcelain, ca. 1925, German, 4⅜"h; 6159 incised on bottom; D; $325.00 – 375.00.

Plate 296. Art Deco cat with ball, same as #101 except 4"h; C; $150.00 – 200.00.

Plate 297. Cat on radio, low fired pottery, ca. 1930, Mexico(?), 6¼"h; very fragile and a charmer; D; $150.00 – 175.00.

Plate 298. Cat with basket of grapes, porcelain, ca. 1915, Germany, 3"h; 760 incised on bottom; D; $250.00 – 350.00.

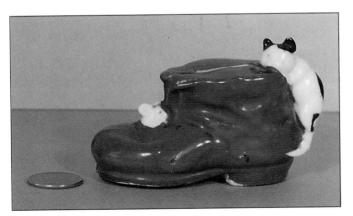

Plate 299. Cat and mouse on shoe, same as #101 except 2½"h; B; $90.00 – 120.00.

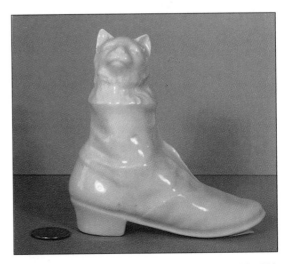

Plate 300. Cat in shoe, porcelain, ca. 1930, US, 5⅞"h; C; $125.00 – 160.00.

Plate 301. Cats (?) in egg, same as #54 except 3¾"h; 1333 incised on bottom; C; $150.00 – 175.00.

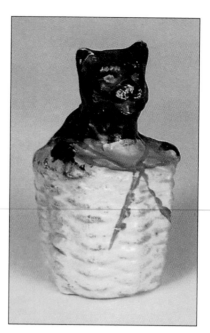

Plate 302. Cat in basket, redware, ca. 1890, US, 3⅞"h; easily chipped and most specimens are; other colors; B; $150.00 – 200.00.

Plate 303. Cats in bag, porcelain, ca. 1925, German; D; $200.00 – 275.00.

Plate 304. Comic cat next to house, same as #101 except C; $125.00 – 150.00.

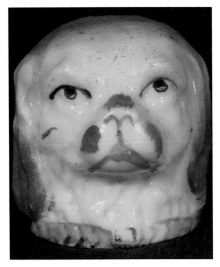

Plate 305. Spaniel head, same as #44 except D; $325.00 – 375.00.

Plate 306. Boxer head, same as #44 except 2"h; C; $250.00 – 300.00.

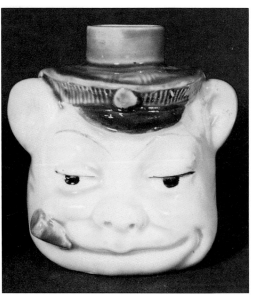

Plate 307. Caricatured dog's head with hat, same as #2 except D; $250.00 – 300.00.

Plate 308. Comic dog's head, same as #101 except C; $125.00 – 150.00.

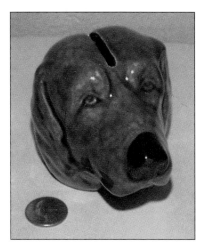

Plate 309. Hound's head, pottery, ca. 1920, English(?), 3¼"h; slightly footed; C; $200.00 – 250.00.

Plate 310. Spaniel head, same as #54 except D; $175.00 – 250.00.

Plate 311. Spaniel head, same as #54(?) except D; $200.00 – 250.00.

Plate 312. Spaniel head, pottery, ca. 1890, English, Staffordshire, 3¾"h; these heads go back to eighteenth century and the early ones look quite primitive; others, like #313, while originating in the Stafforshire region, are very modern and are, therefore, worth only a few dollars; be very cautious in purchasing spaniel heads; D; $350.00 – 400.00.

Plate 313. Spaniel head, pottery contemporary, English, Staffforshire, 4⅛"h; modern editions still available new at this writing. Worth less than $20.00.

Plate 314. Spaniel head, pottery, ca. 1890, English, Staffordshire, 3⅝"h; various colors some with gold highlights, C; $225.00 – 275.00.

Plate 315. Spaniel head, pottery, ca. 1890, English, Staffordshire, 3⅞"h; nice example of flint enamel glaze; various colors; C; $225.00 – 275.00.

Plate 316. Spaniel head, pottery, ca. 1860, English, Rockingham, 3⅞"h; D; $300.00 – 350.00.

Plate 317. Scotty head with purse, same as #101 except 3⅝"h; B; $85.00 – 110.00.

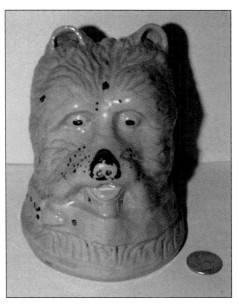

Plate 318. Scotty head on pedestal, pottery, ca. 1920(?), Europe(?); D; $200.00 – 250.00.

Plate 319. Scotty head, same as #54 except 3¼"h; incised on bottom 1015 or 1075; $150.00 – 175.00.

Plate 320. Dog's(?) head, same as #54 except D; $200.00 – 250.00.

Plate 321. Dog wearing fez and coat, same as #54.

Plate 322. Dog's head with bowtie, same as #101 except 3"h; B; $95.00 – 120.00.

Plate 323. Bulldog head, pottery, ca. 1920(?), 2⅜"h; D; $175.00 – 225.00.

Plate 324. Bulldog head with cap, pottery, ca. 1920(?); D; $225.00 – 275.00.

Plate 325. Bulldog head, pottery, ca. 1925, English(?), Rockingham(?), 3"h; C; $150.00 – 200.00.

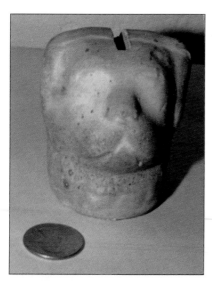

Plate 326. Bulldog(?) head, stoneware, ca. 1910(?), US, 2¾"h; D; $175.00 – 200.00.

Plate 327. Retriever head, porcelain, ca. 1915, Germany, 3¼"h; souvenir of Haverhil, Mass.; gold lettered on head; C; $150.00 – 175.00.

Plate 328. Labrador retriever(?), same as #54 except 3"h; other sizes known; $140.00 – 175.00.

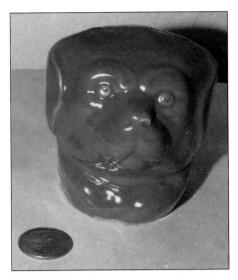

Plate 329. Labrador retriever(?), pottery, ca. 1920, England(?), 3¼"h; D; $175.00 – 200.00.

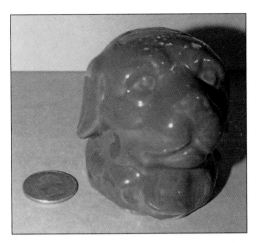

Plate 330. Labrador retriever(?), porcelain, ca. 1920, Germany(?), 2⅝"h; D; $175.00 – 200.00.

Plate 331. Dog's head, same as #273 except 3¾"h; D; $275.00 – 350.00.

Plate 332. Dog's head, porcelain, ca. 1925, Germany(?), 3"h; D; $200.00 – 250.00.

Plate 333. Dachshund, pottery, ca. 1930, US(?); C; $150.00 – 175.00.

Plate 334. Scotty, same as #101 except 5"h; Mt Fuji symbol on bottom; comes in white, black, black and white, and lusterware; A; $40.00 – 50.00.

Plate 335. Scotty, same as #101 except 3⅛"h; C; $125.00 – 150.00.

Plate 336. Scotty, same as #101 except 5"h; Mt. Fuji symbol; B; $75.00 – 100.00.

Plate 337. Scotty, same as #101 except 3⅛"h; B; $75.00 – 100.00.

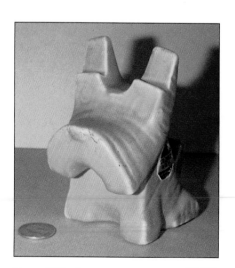

Plate 338. Scotty, pottery, ca. 1935, US Tudor Potteries, Hollywood Ware, LA, CA, 4¾"h; D; $175.00 – 225.00.

Plate 339. Terrier, same as #101 except 4¼"h; B; $75.00 – 100.00.

Plate 340. Terrier, porcelain, ca. 1930, Czechoslovakia, 4"h; C; $125.00 – 150.00.

Plate 341. Terrier with bow, same as #101 except 5"h; A; $50.00 – 75.00.

Plate 342. Terrier, porcelain, ca. 1925, Europe(?), 3¼"h; KLT and O and Masonic symbol on bottom; D; $175.00 – 200.00.

Plate 343. Terrier looking down, same as #101 except C; $125.00 – 150.00.

Plate 344. Terrier leaning forward, pottery majolica, ca. 1930, Czech, 3¾"h; C; $150.00 – 225.00.

Plate 346. Bulldog, same as #101 except 4⅛"h; C; $100.00 – 135.00.

Plate 345. Bulldog, same as #273 except 2½"h; C; $250.00 – 375.00.

Plate 347. Bulldog with BB eyes, pottery, ca. 1920, English(?), 4½"h; footed base, eyes move like BB games; D; $150.00 – 200.00.

Plate 348. Bulldog with toothache, redware, ca. 1915, US, 4⅜"h; E; $350.00 – 450.00.

Plate 349. Sitting Bulldog, same as #144 except 3"h; C; $150.00 – 175.00.

Plate 350. Bulldog on base, porcelain, ca. 1910, German, 3½"h; incised 7507 Germany; D; $225.00 – 275.00.

Plate 351. Bulldog with pot back, pottery, ca. 1925, US(?), 2¾"h; rear of dog extends up to make a pot; D; $200.00 – 250.00.

Plate 352. Bulldog showing teeth, pottery, ca. 1910, English(?), Rockingham(?), 3⅝"h; C; $150.00 – 175.00.

Plate 353. Bulldog with bib, porcelain, ca. 1930, Czech 4¼"h; possibly an ACP (#144) product; C; $175.00 – 200.00.

Plate 354. Bulldog in coat, same as #2 except $175.00 – 200.00.

Plate 355. Bulldog on square base, pottery, ca. 1910, English(?), Rockingham(?), 7⅜"h; D; $275.00 – 300.00.

Plate 356. Bulldog(?), pottery, ca. 1920, European(?); C; $150.00 – 175.00.

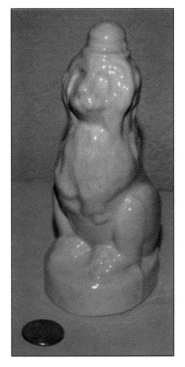

Plate 357. Spaniel with hat, pottery, ca. 1920, English(?), 6⅜"h, oval footed base; C; $175.00 – 200.00.

Plate 358. Spaniel on oval base, pottery, ca. 1900, English(?), 5¼"h; D; $250.00 – 300.00.

Plate 359. Spaniels (right and left), pottery, ca. 1890, English Rockingham, 4⅞"h; D; $250.00 – 300.00 each.

Plate 360. Seated spaniel with chain, pottery, ca. 1890, English Rockingham or Staffordshire, 9⅛"h; this version is found in white but ordinarily not as a bank; unusual coin slot in base in this piece, but cut before glaze; probably a special order; E; $350.00 – 500.00.

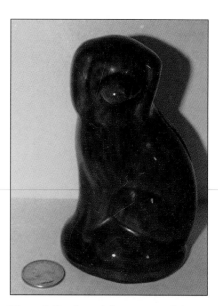

Plate 361. Spaniel on round base, pottery, ca. 1900, English(?), Rockingham or Staffordshire(?) 4⅞"h; C; $175.00 – 225.00.

Plate 362. Wolfhound, same as #144 except 4⅜"h; this one and #363 offer distinction between usually smaller tan version and larger usually colored version; C; $150.00 – 175.00.

Plate 363. Wolfhound, same as #144 except porcelain colored version, 5¼"h; see #362; D; $350.00 – 450.00.

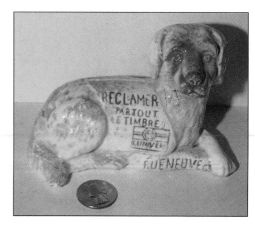

Plate 364. Retriever, pottery, ca. 1920, French, 3⅜"h; French dog food ad for Lunvers on side of dog; D; $250.00 – 275.00.

Plate 353. Bulldog with bib, porcelain, ca. 1930, Czech 4¼"h; possibly an ACP (#144) product; C; $175.00 – 200.00.

Plate 354. Bulldog in coat, same as #2 except $175.00 – 200.00.

Plate 355. Bulldog on square base, pottery, ca. 1910, English(?), Rockingham(?), 7⅜"h; D; $275.00 – 300.00.

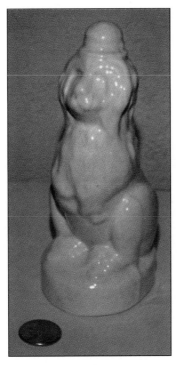

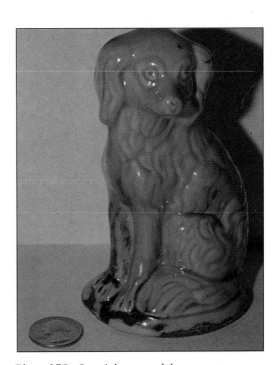

Plate 356. Bulldog(?), pottery, ca. 1920, European(?); C; $150.00 – 175.00.

Plate 357. Spaniel with hat, pottery, ca. 1920, English(?), 6⅜"h, oval footed base; C; $175.00 – 200.00.

Plate 358. Spaniel on oval base, pottery, ca. 1900, English(?), 5¼"h; D; $250.00 – 300.00.

Plate 359. Spaniels (right and left), pottery, ca. 1890, English Rockingham, 4⅞"h; D; $250.00 – 300.00 each.

Plate 360. Seated spaniel with chain, pottery, ca. 1890, English Rockingham or Staffordshire, 9⅛"h; this version is found in white but ordinarily not as a bank; unusual coin slot in base in this piece, but cut before glaze; probably a special order; E; $350.00 – 500.00.

Plate 361. Spaniel on round base, pottery, ca. 1900, English(?), Rockingham or Staffordshire(?) 4⅞"h; C; $175.00 – 225.00.

Plate 362. Wolfhound, same as #144 except 4⅜"h; this one and #363 offer distinction between usually smaller tan version and larger usually colored version; C; $150.00 – 175.00.

Plate 363. Wolfhound, same as #144 except porcelain colored version, 5¼"h; see #362; D; $350.00 – 450.00.

Plate 364. Retriever, pottery, ca. 1920, French, 3⅜"h; French dog food ad for Lunvers on side of dog; D; $250.00 – 275.00.

Plate 365. Retriever, pottery, ca. 1910, US(?), 2¾"h; D; $275.00 – 325.00.

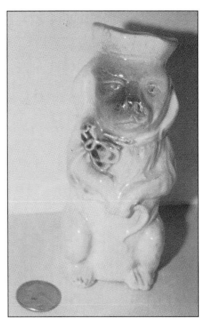

Plate 366. Retriever type dog with hat and bow, majolica, ca. 1925, same as #2(?), 5⅝"h; C; $225.00 – 275.00.

Plate 367. Dog with red coat, same as #2 except 4¾"h; 8822 incised on bottom; C; $225.00 – 275.00.

Plate 368. Police dog(?), pottery, ca. 1935, US(?), 5"h; crudely made and decorated; D; $175.00 – 200.00.

Plate 369. Hound, same as #144 except C; $150.00 – 175.00.

Plate 370. Short haired dog, pottery, ca. 1910, US(?); D; $200.00 – 225.00.

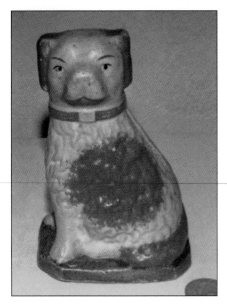

Plate 371. Curly haired dog, pottery, ca. 1880, US(?); E; $300.00 – 350.00.

Plate 372. Fido, same as #101 except 4¼"h; B; $125.00 – 150.00.

Plate 373. Comic dog with cocked head, same as #101 except 3⅛"h; marked with elephant head symbol; B; $100.00 – 125.00.

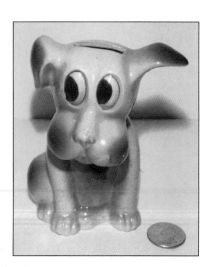

Plate 374. Comic dog, same as #101 except 2¾"h; various colors; A; $50.00 – 60.00.

Plate 375. Sitting comic dog, same as #101 except 4¾"h; various colors; A; $50.00 – 60.00.

Plate 376. Comic dog playing mandolin, same as #101 except 4½"h; B; $85.00 – 100.00.

Plate 377. Comic spaniel, pottery, ca. 1940, US, 3¾"h; B; $75.00 – 100.00.

Plate 378. Strange dog, pottery, ca. 1910(?), US; C; $125.00 – 150.00.

Plate 379. Whiskered comic dog, same as #101 except 3⅛"h; decal says, "Souvenir of Niagra Falls"; C; $100.00 – 125.00.

Plate 380. Comic dog with basket, same as #101 except 3¾"h; C; $125.00 – 150.00.

Plate 381. Comic dog with toothache, same as #101 except 3⅞"h; C; $125.00 – 150.00.

Plate 382. Comic mechanical dog, same as #294, 5"h at rear of body; E; $300.00 – 400.00.

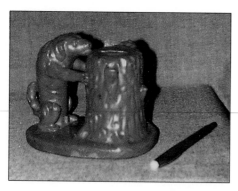

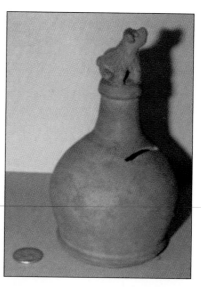

Plate 383. Dog at stump, glazed redware, ca. 1850, US, Pennsylvania redware folk art 5⅜"h (described and priced by Sidney Gecker); F; $1,400.00 – 1,600.00.

Plate 384. Dog at dog house, glazed redware, ca. 1850, US, Pennsylvania redware folk art 3⅛"h (described and priced by Sidney Gecker); F; $1,100.00 – 1,300.00.

Plate 385. Dog finial on jug, unglazed redware, ca. 1840, US, Pennsylvania redware folk art(?) 7¼"h; F; $800.00 – 1,000.00.

Plate 386. Dog lunging from doghouse, porcelain (plus wood and metal), ca. 1900, English(?), 3⅞"h; D; $225.00 – 275.00.

Plate 387. Dog guarding doghouse, porcelain (plus cardboard and seashells), ca. 1890, English, 3⅞"h; "Beware of the Dog" on one side; these seashell creations are called Sailors' Valentines and were popular around the turn of century; D; $225.00 – 275.00.

Plate 388. Bulldog in doghouse, same as #144 except C; $150.00 – 175.00.

Plate 389. Bulldog guarding poke, same as #233 except D; $225.00 – 275.00.

Plate 390. Bulldog climbing on drum, same as #233 except D; $225.00 – 275.00.

Plate 391. Bulldog(?) on box, pottery, ca. 1870, English(?), Staffordshire(?), 2⅛"h; D; $225.00 – 275.00.

Plate 392. Pups in a box, same as #54 except C; $150.00 – 175.00.

Plate 393. Spaniel sleeping in doghouse, same as #144 except colored version; also comes in brown or tan (rated B; $100.00 – 125.00) and in various sizes, C; $150.00 – 175.00.

Plate 394. Adult dog with pups on books, porcelain, overpainted, ca. 1930, Japan, 4½"h; others animals in this series; C; $125.00 – 150.00.

Plate 395. Spaniel on ornate base, stoneware, ca. 1875, US, 2⅝"h; E; $300.00 – 375.00.

Plate 396. Spaniel on fringed stool, pottery, ca. 1880, European(?); D; $200.00 – 275.00.

Plate 397. Spaniel on mantel, pottery, ca. 1910, English, 4"h; footed; D; $200.00 – 250.00.

Plate 400. Pup in a poke, same as #54(?) except C; $150.00 – 175.00.

Plate 398. Spaniel on crossed box, pottery, ca. 1890, English(?), 2"h; C; $175.00 – 225.00.

Plate 399. Two pups(?) in a poke, porcelain, ca. 1920, German, 3¾"h; 5848 incised on rear; C; $175.00 – 200.00.

Plate 401. Scotty playing a drum, same as #101 except 3¼"h; possibly toothbrush holder instead of bank; B; $75.00 – 100.00.

Plate 402. Dog in doghouse, pottery, ca. 1925, European(?), 3⅛"h; C; $100.00 – 125.00.

Plate 403. Comic dog by doghouse, same as #101 except C; $100.00 – 125.00.

Plate 404. Dog by purse, porcelain, ca. 1925, German(?); C; $150.00 – 175.00.

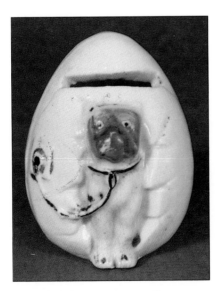

Plate 405. Dog guarding egg, porcelain(?), ca. 1920, German(?); C; $150.00 – 200.00.

Plate 406. Dog wheel toy, same as #101 except C; $135.00 – 165.00.

Plate 407. Dog pulling cart, same as #54 except D; $275.00 – 300.00.

Elephants

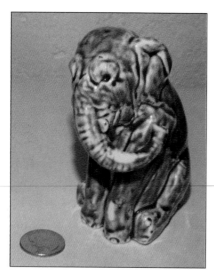

Plate 408. Seated elephant, porcelain same as #144 except 4¼"h; C; $150.00 – 200.00.

Plate 409. Elephant with raised trunk, same as #101 except 3⅜"h; the raised trunk is an Oriental symbol of good luck and one of our favorites; these come with various colors and decorations, the monochromes are scarcer; C; $150.00 – 200.00.

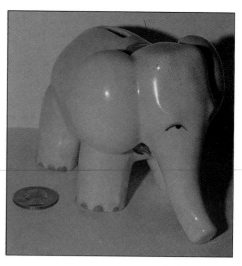

Plate 410. Comic elephant, same as #101 except Fuji symbol, 3⅝"h; C; $110.00 – 125.00.

Plate 411. Elephant in tall grass, pottery, ca. 1925, US, 7⅜"h; the metal KLT coin box sits inside the elephant and is attached to the bottom with a movable flange; C; $150.00 – 200.00.

Plate 412. Lumpy elephant, stoneware, ca. 1935, German, 2⅞"h; has metal KLT inscribed, "Die Sparkasse (The Savings Bank) en Bremen"; C; $150.00 – 175.00.

Plate 413. Standing elephant, pottery, ca. 1935, US, 3¾"h; 46' C3 inscribed on bottom; C; $100.00 – 125.00.

Plate 414. Angry elephant, pottery, ca. 1935, Japan, 4"h; C; $100.00 – 120.00.

Plate 415. Small elephant, porcelain, ca. 1920, Germany(?), 2⅜"h; C; $125.00 – 150.00.

Plate 416. Trumpeting elephant, pottery, ca. 1935, US(?), 5½"h; B; $75.00 – 100.00.

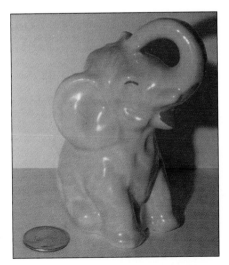

Plate 417. Seated elephant (nearly identical to Vanio version — Moore #461), pottery, ca. 1940, US, 4½"h; B; $75.00 – 90.00.

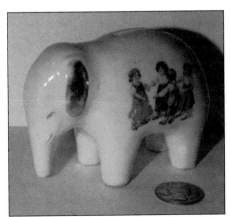

Plate 418. Stylized elephant, porcelain, ca. 1910, German, 3"h; comes with various decorations; C; $150.00 – 175.00.

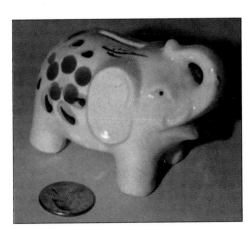

Plate 419. Flowered elephant, porcelain, ca. 1950, Occupied Japan, 2¼"h; B; $75.00 – 100.00.

Plate 420. GOP elephant, pottery, ca. 1890, US, 3¾"h; E; $300.00 – 350.00.

Plate 421. Lumpy elephant, stoneware, ca. 1900, US, 3¾"h; B; $125.00 – 150.00.

Plate 422. Tiny elephant, porcelain, ca. 1915, German, 2"h; D; $175.00 – 200.00.

Plate 423. Political elephant, porcelain, ca. 1910, European, from 1¾"h to 2⅞"h; this elephant has one companion, a similar donkey (#431) and they are believed by most collectors to be Republican and Democrat symbols; C (small); $150.00 – 200.00; D (medium and large); $200.00 – 300.00.

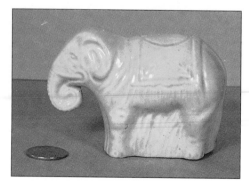

Plate 424. Elephant with blanket, same as #54 except 2¾"h; other versions exist; B; $100.00 – 125.00.

Plate 425. Elephant with saddle, porcelain bisque, ca. 1920, German, 3¾"h; 2872 incised; variations are known; C; $150.00 – 200.00.

Plate 426. Elephant with lock, porcelain, ca. 1920, German, 3⅜"h; C; $150.00 – 200.00.

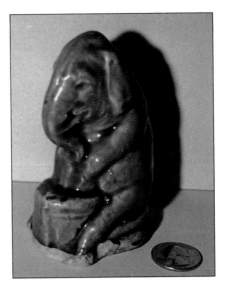

Plate 427. Elephant at tub, pottery, ca. 1910, English(?); D; $150.00 – 200.00.

Plate 428. Elephant on books, same as #394 except 4½"h; C; $125.00 – 150.00.

Plate 429. Timid Elmer Elephant, same as #101 except 5"h; pre-Mickey Mouse Disney character sought after by Disney collectors; note trunk tied on with string; D; $700.00 – 900.00.

Plate 430. Elephant in tutu, pottery, ca. 1940, US; B; $75.00 – 90.00.

Plate 431. Political donkey, same as #423 except 1⅞"h to 3⅛"h; somewhat scarcer than elephant because ears break off easily.

Plate 432. Kicking donkey, porcelain bisque, ca. 1925, Germany, 3⅝"h; 10314 incised; C; $175.00 – 225.00.

Plate 433. Donkey with halter, pottery, ca. 1930, US(?), 5⅝"h; D; $150.00 – 175.00.

Plate 434. Pack mule, same as #101 except 3¼"h; larger size and in another color exist; A; $50.00 – 60.00.

Plate 435. Saddled horse, low fired pottery, ca. 1925, Mexican, 5⅜"h; 1928 written in pen on bottom; very fragile; E; $225.00 – 275.00.

Plate 436. Broken-down nag, same as #101 except 3⅜"h; there is a larger size; A; $40.00 – 60.00.

Plate 437. Stylized horse, porcelain, ca. 1950, Occupied Japan, 3¼"h; B; $75.00 – 100.00.

Plate 438. Rocking horse, pottery, ca. 1940, US, 4⅝"h; C; $100.00 – 125.00.

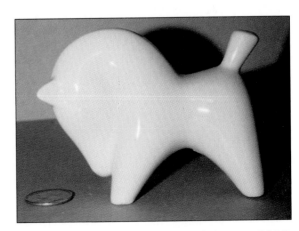

Plate 439. Deco horse, porcelain, ca. 1935, Japan(?), 3"h; D; $200.00 – 250.00.

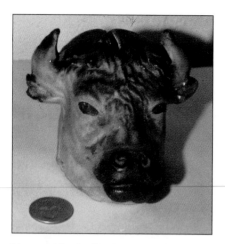

Plate 440. Bull's head, pottery, ca. 1920 US 3¼"h (same as Moore #538); C; $175.00 – 200.00.

Plate 441. Bull's head, same as #54 except 3¼"h; C; $150.00 – 200.00.

Plate 442. Cow on base, pottery, ca. 1890, Swiss, 3½" (see notes #286); E; $400.00 – 500.00.

Plate 443. Reclining cow, bisque pottery (possibly heavy porcelain), ca. 1890, German, 2¼"h; 6414 incised on bottom; "gift to mother 1890, Selena Barnett Wayland born June 10, 1888 Coversville, Va." written on bottom; E; $300.00 – 400.00.

Plate 444. Comic cow, pottery, ca. 1940, US; B; $75.00 – 100.00.

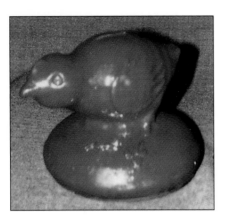

Plate 445. Chick and worm, redware, ca. 1850, US, Pennsylvania folk art, 4½"h (described and priced by Sidney Gecker); "April 4, 1861" penciled on bottom; E; $800.00 – 1,200.00.

Plate 446. Easter chick, same as #54 except 3¾"h; "Easter" molded on side; 1406 incised on bottom; C; $150.00 – 175.00.

Plate 447. Chick busting out of shell, same as #54; C; $150.00 – 175.00.

Plate 448. Rooster crowing, majolica, ca. 1910, European(?); D; $200.00 – 250.00.

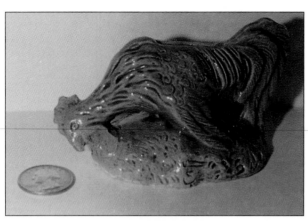

Plate 449. Rooster displaying, same as #54 except 2½"h; C; $125.00 – 150.00.

Plate 450. Chicken head, low fired pottery, ca. 1920, Mexican(?), 3⅝"h; C; $100.00 – 125.00.

Plate 451. Stylized Chicken, pottery, ca. 1920, European(?); D; $200.00 – 250.00.

Plate 452. Chicken on oval base, pottery, ca. 1840, US, Pennsylvania folk art, 6"h (described and priced by Sidney Gecker); part of comb broken off; E; $1,000.00 – 1,400.00.

Plate 453. Chicken on round base, low fired pottery, ca. 1920, Mexican(?); C; $100.00 – 125.00.

Plate 454. Chicken on base, redware, ca. 1860, US(?); D; $200.00 – 250.00.

Plate 455. Chicken on pedestal, same as #144 except 5⅝"h; only known in colored versions; B; $100.00 – 125.00.

Plate 456. Italian chicken, pottery, ca. 1910, Italian(?), 4⅞"h; D; $200.00 – 250.00.

Plate 457. Spattered chicken, pottery, ca. 1890, US(?), 7½"h; spatterware glaze; D; $250.00 – 300.00.

Plate 458. Scroddleware chicken, scroddled redware, ca. 1880, US(?), 3¼"h; D; $250.00 – 300.00.

Plate 459. Chicken on nest, pottery, ca. 1900, US(?), 5"h; D; $250.00 – 300.00.

Plate 460. Chicken on nest, pottery or stoneware, ca. 1900, US(?), 3⅞"h; C; $125.00 – 150.00.

Plate 461. Chicken on nest, pottery, ca. 1900, US(?), 3⅜"h; C; $125.00 – 150.00.

Plate 462. Chicken on nest with chicks, pottery, ca. 1930(?), Guatemala, 3⅜"h; C; $125.00 – 150.00.

Plate 463. Primitive chicken on nest, redware, ca. 1880(?), US(?), 3⅛"h; coin slot is ⁹⁄₁₆" long and will not accommodate any contemporary coin; could handle several nineteenth century coins; D; $150.00 – 175.00.

Buffalos

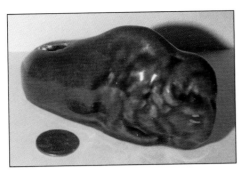

Plate 464. Sleeping buffalo, pottery with Rockingham glaze, ca. 1890, US(?), 2⅝"h; D; $225.00 – 275.00.

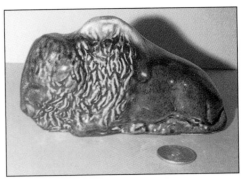

Plate 465. Expo 1901 buffalo, pottery, ca. 1900, US, Roseville, 3¼"h; "Expo 1901" on rear; souvenir for 1901 Buffalo, NY Exposition; D; $300.00 – 400.00.

Plate 466. Resting buffalo, pottery, ca. 1900, US, Roseville, 3"h; slot in bottom; several glaze variations known; C; $150.00 – 175.00.

Plate 467. Standing buffalo, pottery, ca. 1920, US, 2¾"h; several others with similar glaze known, maker unknown; D; $225.00 – 250.00.

Plate 468. Standing buffalo, porcelain, ca. 1930, US(?); D; $200.00 – 225.00.

Plate 469. Buffalo with pants, porcelain, ca. 1920, Germany; D; $225.00 – 250.00.

Plate 470. Reclining Rabbit, same as #144 two sizes known, 2"h; C; $150.00, and 2¾"h; D; $275.00.

Plate 471. Birth Rabbit, pottery, ca. 1925, Japan, 2⅝"h; see Japanese rabbit bank in text; E; $275.00 – 300.00.

Plate 472. Floppy-eared rabbit, pottery, ca. 1930, US, 3⅝"h; C; $250.00 – 175.00.

Plate 473. Crouching rabbit, same as #54 except 2¼"h; B; $100.00 – 125.00.

Plate 474. Long-eared rabbit, pottery, ca. 1930, US, 2⅞"h; C; $100.00 – 125.00.

Plate 475. Rabbit on base, Faience (majolica) redware, ca. 1890, France, 2¾"h; E; $350.00 – 400.00.

Plate 476. Sitting rabbit, pottery, ca. 1930, Italian(?), 3½"h; "Fornai" on bottom; D; $200.00 – 225.00.

Plate 477. Rabbit with whistle, low fired pottery, ca. 1910, Mexico, over 6"h; note whistle included in front base, a common Mexican folk art device; D; $200.00 – 225.00.

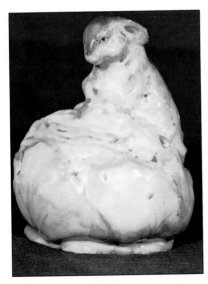

Plate 478. Rabbit at cabbage, porcelain, ca. 1920, German(?); C; $175.00 – 200.00.

Plate 479. Rabbit with coat, hat, and cane, same as #144 porcelain, marked Austria; comes in three sizes, 4¼"h (brown and black), A, $85.00 – 110.00; 4⅝"h (color), C; $150.00 – 175.00; 5⅛"h (color); D; $225.00 – 250.00.

Plate 480. Van Dyke rabbit, same as #144 pottery, ca. 1910, 3⅝"h; "VAN DYKE TEAS, OUR OWN STORES EVERYWHERE"; marked Austria; C; $150.00 – 175.00.

Pigs

Pigs are the most common subject for ceramic coin banks. Generally they are more plentiful and lower priced with few exceptions, such as #481. Their numbers have been reduced as much as possible.

Plate 481. Pig's head, same as #44 except 1¾"h; E; $375.00 – 450.00.

Plate 482. Pig's head with high hat, same as #54(?) except 3½"h; D; $200.00 – 250.00.

Plate 483. Pig's head with small hat, same as #54 except 3⅛"h; C; $150.00 – 175.00.

Plate 484. Comic pig's head, same as #101 except 3⅞"h; C; $100.00 – 125.00.

Plate 485. Comic pig's head with bow, same as #101 except 3⅛"h; B; $65.00 – 85.00.

Plate 486. Tiny pig, same as #101 except 2"h (probably the most common ceramic coin bank); A; $20.00 – 30.00.

Plate 487. Luster pig, porcelain with lusterware glaze, ca. 1930, Czech, 2⅜"h; C; $110.00 – 130.00.

Plate 488. Plain pig, pottery, ca. 1900, US(?), 2"h; C; $110.00 – 130.00.

Plate 489. Pig on grass base, pottery, ca. 1910, Germany(?), 2⅜"h; C; $120.00 – 140.00.

Plate 490. Deco pig, heavy porcelain, ca. 1935, Czech, 2⅞"h; B; $75.00 – 85.00.

Plate 491. Sleeping pig, pottery, ca. 1915, European(?); C; $100.00 – 120.00.

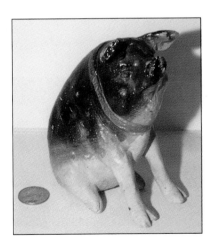

Plate 492. Sitting pig, low fired pottery, ca. 1930, Mexican, 5"h; B; $60.00 – 70.00.

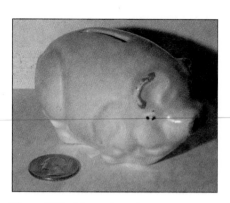

Plate 493. Muscular pig, pottery, ca. 1935, Japan, 2¼"h; a variety of colors exist, made for many years; A; $25.00 – 35.00.

Plate 494. Plain pig, pottery, ca. 1930, US, 3¼"h; D; $150.00 – 175.00.

Plate 495. Resting pig, same as #144 except porcelain, 1⅝"h; C; $120.00 – 130.00.

Plate 496. Resting pig, too, same as #54 except 2⅜"h; B; $90.00 – 110.00.

Plate 497. Stylized pig, pottery, ca. 1935, Chinese; D; $150.00 – 175.00.

Plate 498. Sitting pig, same as #54 except D; $175.00 – 200.00.

Plate 499. Black pig, pottery, ca. 1930, English, 2¾"h; Made in England and 1132 incised on bottom; A; $65.00 – 75.00.

Plate 500. Cute standing pig, pottery, ca. 1940, USA; A; $40.00 – 50.00.

Plate 501. Common pig, same as #101 except comes in sizes from 1¾"h to 3⅜"h, mostly pink, some with bows (#502), some with handles, and a few in lusterware; all are A with a few near B; $20.00 – 75.00.

Plate 502. Common pig with bow, see #501.

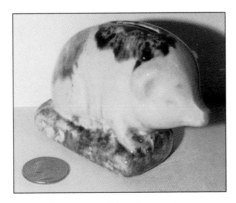

Plate 503. Roseville pig on base, same as #273 except 2⅞"h; thought to be the oldest Roseville pig, ca. 1910; C; $150.00 – 200.00.

Plate 504. Razor Back pig, pottery, ca. 1925, US, Roseville, 3⅛"h; C; usually without razor back rated A; $125.00 – 150.00.

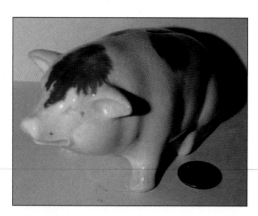

Plate 505. Roseville Pig, same as #504 except 3⅛"h; A; $75.00 – 100.00.

Plate 506. McCoy pig, pottery, ca. 1930, US, McCoy, 3"h; comes more often in reverse colors; many have USA on rear bellies; some authors have identified McCoys as Roseville; note narrow pointed snout on Roseville and short blunt snout on McCoy; A; $50.00 – 75.00.

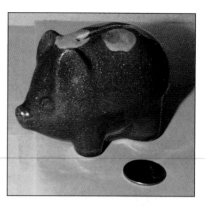

Plate 507. Little McCoy pig, same as #506 except not as long and 2¾"h.

Plate 508. McCoy pig with head turned, same as #506 except 3⅞"h.

Plate 509. Hole-eyed pig, pottery, ca. 1880 – 1920, Austrian Empire, 2¼"h, A; $35.00 – 65.00. Some, as one shown, have advertising and are scarcer and higher priced. Medium size B; $75.00 – 100.00. Large size 4"h; C; $125.00 – 175.00.

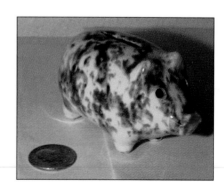

Plate 510. Cambridge hole-eyed pig, pottery, ca. 1910, US, Cambridge Art Pottery, Cambridge, Ohio, 2⅛"h (varies); these come in spatterware (shown) and several drip glazes; B; $120.00 – 140.00.

Plate 511. Hole-eyed pig with no holes, pottery, ca. 1880 – 1920, US, 2⅝"h; "Souvenir of Big Rapids, Mich" gold lettered on side; B; $75.00 – 100.00.

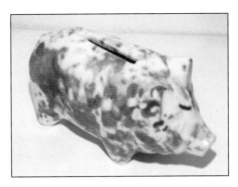

Plate 512. Hole-eyed pig with no holes, same as #511 except spatterware, 2¼"h.

Plate 513. Hole-eyed pig with no holes, same as #511 except drip glaze yellow ware, 2½"h.

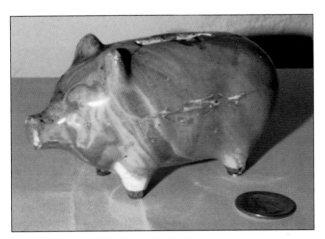

Plate 514. Hole-eyed pig with no holes, same as #511 except marbled drip glaze, 2½"h.

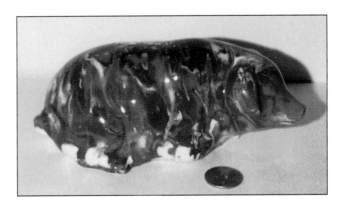

Plate 515. Marbled pig, pottery, ca. 1920, US, 2¾"h; C; $100.00 – 125.00.

Plate 516. Pig standing, porcelain bisque, ca. 1920, German, 2"h; B; $100.00 – 125.00.

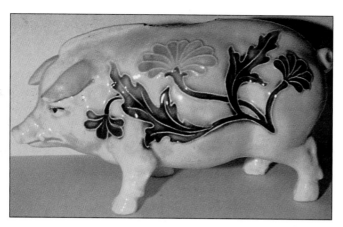

Plate 517. Pig with ornate flowers, majolica, ca. 1925, Czech, 3"h; 6507 and 97 incised on stomach; C; $150.00 – 175.00.

Plate 518. Souvenir pig, porcelain, ca. 1910, German, 2½"h; comes with various decorations and souvenir inscriptions. "State House, Boston" shown; B; $85.00 – 110.00.

Plate 519. Standing pig, pottery, ca. 1930, Czech, 2⅞"h; C; $90.00 – 110.00.

Plate 520. Heinold pig, pottery, ca. 1940, US, 2⅝"h; inscribed "Heinold Hog Markets"; B; $75.00 – 100.00.

Plate 521. Round pig, pottery, ca. 1935, US, 2¾"h; has various inscriptions, this one with Hanover coat of arms; B; $65.00 – 75.00.

Plate 522. Delft pig, majolica, ca. 1940, Netherlands; A; $50.00 – 75.00.

Plate 523. Pig with handle, low fired pottery, ca. 1940, Mexico, 2¾"h; larger later versions are common; A; $35.00 – 45.00.

Plate 524. Lumpy pig, same as #523 except ca. 1930, 4"h; B; $65.00 – 75.00.

Plate 525. Pig with squares, same as #101 except C; two sizes known; $125.00 – 150.00.

Plate 526. Painted pig, pottery with overpaint, ca. 1940, McCoy, 2⅞"h; overpaint often nearly gone; A; $55.00 – 70.00.

Plate 527. Fat pig, stoneware, ca. 1930, US, 2½"h; C; $95.00 – 110.00.

Plate 528. Lumpy pig, same as #101 except A; $55.00 – 65.00.

Plate 529. Ballooned pig, same as #101 except A; $40.00 – 50.00.

Plate 530. Round pig, same as #101 except A; $40.00 – 50.00.

Plate 531. Common pig, same as #101 except Occupied Japan; A; $35.00 – 45.00.

Plate 532. Pig with bow, same as #531.

Plate 533. Thin pig, pottery, ca. 1940, US, 3"h; A; $65.00 – 75.00.

Plate 534. Triangular pig, same as #101 except 2½"h; B; $65.00 – 75.00.

PIGS

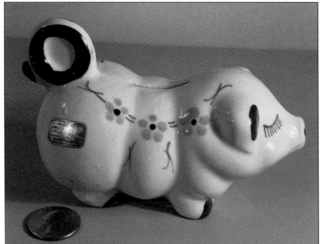

Plate 535. Pig with handle tail, pottery, ca. 1935, US, Rio Hondo Potteries, El Monte, California, 3⅜"h; the rise of cute animals, many of them pigs, began in the 1930s, perhaps to cheer up the Depression milieu, and continued through the 1950s; many of them were made by Rio Hondo, where, incidently, Tom played in their tailings as a child; others are attributed to Shawnee Pottery; B; $75.00 – 85.00.

Plate 536. Guilty pig, same as #535 except 4¼"h.

Plate 537. Pig in work clothes, redware, ca. 1890, US, Pennsylvania folk art 4⅛"h; E; $350.00 – 450.00.

Plate 538. Shy pig, same as #535 except 3¼"h.

Plate 540. Pig on haunches, same as #535(?) except 2¾"h.

Plate 539. Pig with cap, same as #144 except 5⅛"h; larger version probably scarcer than rated; B; $120.00 – 140.00.

117

Plate 541. Porky Pig, porcelain bisque with overpaint, ca. 1935, Japan, 5"h; paint often nearly gone; C; $250.00 – 300.00.

Plate 542. Formal gowned pig, porcelain, ca. 1950, Occupied Japan, 4¼"h; B; $75.00 – 85.00.

Plate 543. Bow tied pig, same as #542 except 4⅜"h.

Plate 544. Pig in suit and vest, same as #542 except 4"h; C; $120.00 – 130.00.

Plate 545. Pig with shinto cap, same as #542 except 4½"h; C; $100.00 – 120.00.

Plate 546. Pig in pajamas, same as #542 except 3⅛"h; D; $175.00 – 200.00.

Plate 547. Pitcher pig, pottery, ca. 1940, US, 3⅞"h; C; $125.00 – 140.00.

Plate 548. Pig with suit and hat, same as #535 except 4⅞"h.

Plate 549. Pig with bonnet, same as #535 except 4⅞"h.

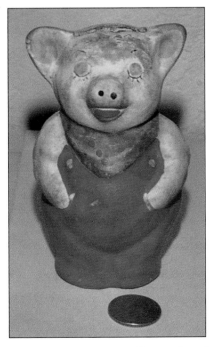

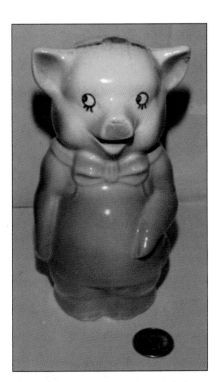

Plate 550. The Wise Pig, pottery, ca. 1935, US, 6⅛"h; there are several versions copying this Hubley iron bank Moore #590; A; $75.00 – 100.00.

Plate 551. Pig in overalls, unglazed pottery, ca. 1935, USA; A; $35.00 – 50.00.

Plate 552. Standing pig with bow, pottery, ca. 1940, USA; A; $35.00 – 45.00.

Plate 553. Cheerful pig, pottery, ca. 1940, USA; A; $35.00 – 45.00.

Plate 554. Smug pig, pottery, ca. 1935, USA; A; $40.00 – 50.00.

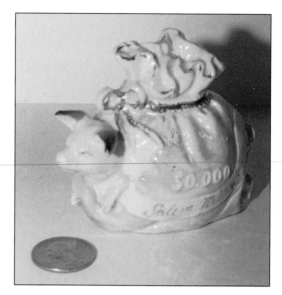

Plate 555. Best pig in poke, porcelain, ca. 1920, Germany, 3"h; 4798 incised; D; $200.00 – 250.00.

Plate 556. Pig in sack poke, porcelain, ca. 1925, Germany, 2⅞"h; "Made In Germany" in circle on back; possible Shafer and Vater (see #233); A; $125.00 – 150.00.

Plate 557. Cheap pig in poke, porcelain, ca. 1925, Germany, 2¾"h; this one in a crude and carelessly made series that mostly parallels the ones illustrated in #556; some have "Made in Germany" incised and most are not shown; A; $50.00 – 60.00.

Plate 558. Pig in purse poke, same as #556 except 2⅝"h; there are several sizes, the larger ones are scarcer and worth more.

Plate 559. Pig in satchel poke, same as #556 except 4⅛"h; only large version known; D; $175.00 – 200.00.

Plate 560. Pig in poke, same as #54 except C; $100.00 – 120.00.

Plate 561. Pig in purse poke, same as #54 except C; $100.00 – 120.00.

Plate 562. Pig in fancy purse poke, same as #54(?) except D; $135.00 – 160.00.

Plate 563. Pig at poke, same as #54 except C; $100.00 – 120.00.

Plate 564. Pig at bag poke, same as #556 except C; $125.00 – 150.00.

Plate 565. Pigs on poke, same as #557.

Plate 566. Pig playing flute with piglets in poke, same as #557 except C; $90.00 – 110.00.

Plate 567. Pig in drum, same as #556 except two sizes, 3"h and 3½"h; C; $120.00 – 140.00; and D; $175.00 – 200.00.

Plate 568. Pig in counting house, porcelain, ca. 1930, Germany, 3¼"h; B; $95.00 – 110.00.

Plate 569. Pig at mail box, same as #557 except 3½"h; B; $85.00 – 95.00.

Plate 570. Pigs playing piano and guitar, same as #557 except 2⅞"h; B; $95.00 – 100.00.

Plate 571. Formal pig with umbrella, pottery, ca. 1900, English(?), 5¼"h; several colors; C; $150.00 – 175.00.

Plate 572. Pig on couch, same as #144 except 2½"h; C; $140.00 – 160.00.

Plate 573. Wide faced pig with collar, redware, ca. 1835, US, Pennsylvania, 5¼"h (described and priced by Sidney Gecker); F; $2,800.00 – 3,200.00.

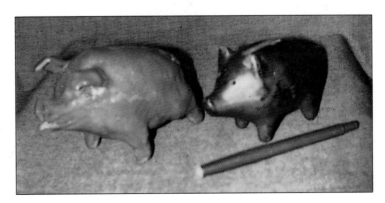

Plate 574. Two small pig banks, redware, ca. 1870, US(?) (described and priced by Sidney Gecker); D; $200.00 – 400.00.

Plate 575. Turkey with feathers folded, same as #144, two colored sizes, 3⅞"h and 5⅛"h; a smaller tan version may exist; inscribed on bottom of large one shown, "Edith, 1 yr. old from Mt Eaton Suni (sic) School Christmas Monroe Co."; B; $150.00 – 175.00; and D; $275.00 – 325.00.

Plate 576. Resting turkey, same as #144, two sizes, 3⅛"h (tan) and 4⅜"h (shown); B; $110.00 – 130.00; and C; $150.00 – 175.00.

Plate 577. Turkey piece, same as #144, 5¼"h; "A Welcome Piece For Our Table" molded on base; other sizes and colors probably exist; C; $150.00 – 175.00.

Plate 578. Turkey displaying, porcelain bisque, ca. 1925, Germany, 4¼"h; a number of finishes and souvenir pieces are known and prices should be based on their desirability; B; $100.00 – 125.00.

Plate 579. Turkey resting, pottery, ca. 1910, US, 3"h; turkey feet are molded on footed bottom; D; $250.00 – 300.00.

Plate 580. Goat's head, porcelain(?), ca. 1915, European; C; $150.00 – 175.00.

Plate 581. Round horn goat's head, same as #54(?) except 2⅜"h; C; $125.00 – 150.00.

Plate 582. Shaggy goat resting, same as #54 except 2⅝"h; 2819 incised on bottom; B; $100.00 – 125.00.

Plate 583. Bearded goat resting, same as #144, two sizes, 3"h (tan) and 3⅞"h (shown); B; $100.00 – 125.00; and C; $175.00 – 200.00.

Plate 584. Smiling goat, porcelain bisque, ca. 1925, Europe(?); 3⅞"h, D; $225.00 – 250.00.

Plate 585. Sheep's head, same as #44 except 1⅞"h; C; $325.00 – 350.00.

Plate 586. Sheep on books, same as #394 except 4¾"h; B; $125.00 – 150.00.

Plate 587. Round horned sheep, same as #54(?) except 2⅞"h; D; $250.00 – 350.00.

Plate 588. Sheep on oval base, pottery, ca. 1890, Europe(?), 3¼"h; E; $350.00 – 450.00.

Plate 589. Sheep with whistle, low fired pottery, ca. 1920, Mexican, 4⅛"h; note whistle on base; D; $200.00 – 250.00.

Plate 590. Cute sheep, pottery, ca. 1935, US, Rio Hondo Potteries(?); B; $75.00 – 100.00.

Plate 591. Owl head, same as #54 except 2⅞"h; C; $135.00 – 160.00.

Plate 592. Owl head with long neck, same as #54 except C; $135.00 – 160.00.

Plate 593. Owl on stump, redware, ca. 1835, US, Pennsylvania, 8⅜"h (priced by Sidney Gecker); F; $3,300.00 – 3,700.00.

Plate 594. Owl turns head, pottery, ca. 1900, US, 6¾"h; based on a well-known Mechanical Bank patented 1880; D; $275.00 – 350.00.

Plate 595. Sad owl, same as #101 except 5⅛"h; C; $120.00 – 140.00.

Plate 596. Owl on rock, same as #144 except 6⅛"h; C; $175.00 – 200.00.

Plate 597. Stiff owl, same as #101 except comes in a variety of sizes from 3⅛"h to 5"h and with numerous glazes and finishes; A; $20.00 – 75.00.

Plate 598. Duck on pedestal, pottery, ca. 1880, US; D; $250.00 – 300.00.

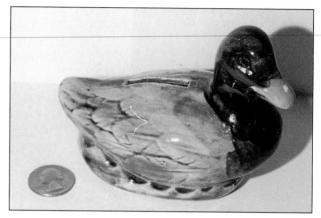

Plate 599. Shiny duck, majolica, ca. 1910, US(?), 3⅝"h; C; $150.00 – 175.00.

Plate 600. Duck on nest, pottery, ca. 1890, US(?), 4"h; footed; D; $225.00 – 250.00.

Plate 601. Duck with handle, pottery, ca. 1920, Italian(?), 4⅝"h; C; $175.00 – 200.00.

Plate 602. Stylized duck, pottery, ca. 1900, US(?), 3"h; C; $150.00 – 175.00.

Plate 603. Duck on oval base, stoneware, ca. 1900, US, 3"h; D; $250.00 – 300.00.

Plate 604. Comic duck, same as #101 except 4⅝"h; "Japan" stamped inside spread eagle outlined on bottom; B; $90.00 – 110.00.

Plate 605. Goose hissing, pottery, ca. 1910, US, 3½"h; C; $150.00 – 175.00.

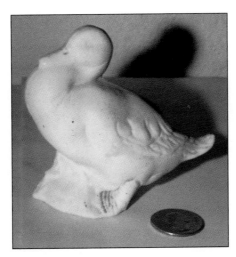

Plate 606. Goose on base, porcelain bisque, ca. 1915, Germany, 3¼"h; B; $100.00 – 125.00.

Plate 607. Goose with ribbon, porcelain, ca. 1920, Europe; D; $200.00 – 250.00.

Plate 608. Swan, pottery, ca. 1925, European, 3⅜"h; C; $140.00 – 180.00.

Plate 609. Swan, same as #144 except 3¼"h; C; $150.00 – 175.00.

Plate 610. Oriental crane, pottery, ca. 1925(?), Japan, 3½"h; C; $175.00 – 200.00.

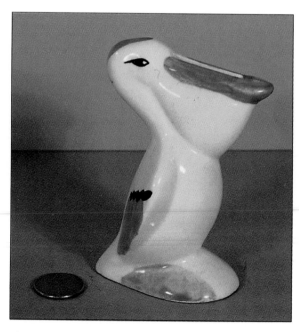

Plate 611. Pelican, pottery, ca. 1935, US, 4½"h; D; $200.00 – 225.00.

Plate 612. Deco pelican, same as #101 except 4½"h; C; $135.00 – 160.00.

Plate 613. Toucan(?), pottery, ca. 1930, Czech, 3⅞"h; D; $175.00 – 200.00.

Plate 614. Eagle's head, same as #273 except 2½"h; C; $175.00 – 225.00.

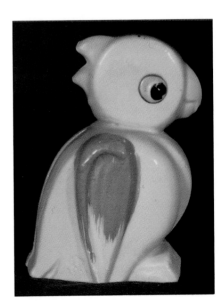

Plate 615. Eagle on pedestal, same as #144 two sizes, 3⅝"h (colored) and 5"h (colored); "MAY HE GIVE US PEACE IN ALL OUR STATES," around base; both C; $200.00 – 250.00.

Plate 616. Parrot leaning, pottery, ca. 1900, US; D; $225.00 – 275.00.

Plate 617. Comic deco parrot, same as #101 except 4⅛"h; diamond shaped manufacturer's mark with flowers in four corners; C; $135.00 – 160.00.

Plate 618. Comic deco albatross, same as #101 except 4¼"h.

Plate 619. Dove, same as #191 except 4½"h; C; $150.00 – 200.00.

Plate 620. Kissing doves, porcelain(?), ca. 1920, European; D; $200.00 – 225.00.

Plate 621. Dove on birdhouse, pottery, ca. 1910, English, Rockingham, 6⅞"h; D; $175.00 – 200.00.

Plate 622. Bird, pottery, ca. 1910, US, 2¾"h; D; $175.00 – 200.00.

Plate 623. Decorated bird, majolica, ca. 1935, Italian(?), 3"h; "Vesto Alobach #245" under the glaze on bottom; C; $150.00 – 175.00.

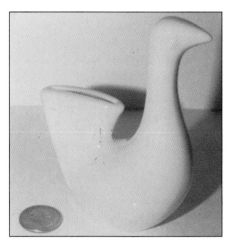

Plate 624. Stylized bird, same as #101(?) except 4⅝"h; D; $150.00 – 175.00.

Plate 625. Peacock, majolica, ca. 1920, European(?), 4⅞"h; C; $200.00 – 225.00.

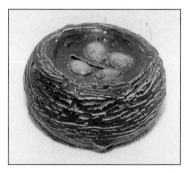

Plate 626. Robin's nest, pottery, ca. 1900, US; C; $175.00 – 200.00.

Plate 627. Urns decorated with birds, pottery, ca. 1860, England, Sussexware, usually 6" to 9"h; E; $300.00 – 500.00.

Plate 628. Birds on branch, pottery, ca. 1880, England, inspired by Sussexware; E; $300.00 – 350.00.

Plate 629. Diorama with bird finial, pottery, ca. 1890, European(?); F; $400.00 – 500.00.

Plate 630. Squirrel eating nut, same as #144 except 4⅜"h; C; $150.00 – 175.00.

Plate 631. Beehive, pottery with drip glaze, ca. 1900, US(?), 2⅝"h; D; $200.00 – 225.00.

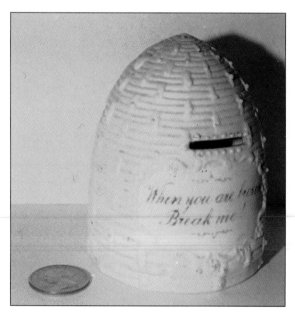

Plate 632. Beehive with motto, porcelain bisque, ca. 1920, German, 3¾"h; 6388 incised on bottom; motto, "When You Are Broken Break Me"; C; $175.00 – 200.00.

Plate 633. Beehive with legs, pottery, ca. 1920, US (possible Roseville), 3⅜"h; round hole in bottom for cork, one of first banks to use this type trap; C; $150.00 – 175.00.

Plate 634. Small beehive, same as #273 except 2½"h; like #633 has round hole for cork; D; $250.00 – 300.00.

Plate 635. Beehive with mouse, same as #144, colored version, 3"h; Austria on strip; D; $225.00 – 250.00.

Plate 636. Mice in bun, pottery, ca. 1925, European(?); D; $200.00 – 225.00.

Plate 637. Frog's head, same #54 except C; $125.00 – 150.00.

Plate 638. Frog, same as #273 except 2⅞"h; C; $225.00 – 250.00.

Plate 639. Sitting frog, same as #273 except 2¾"h; C; $225.00 – 250.00.

Plate 640. Comic frog, same as #101 except overpaint, comes in several sizes starting at 3⅞"h; B; $75.00 – 100.00.

Plate 641. Frog with ribbon, porcelain(?), ca. 1925, European; C; $150.00 – 175.00.

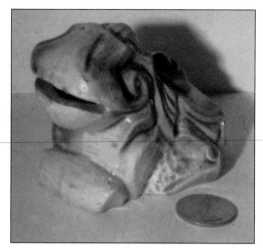

Plate 642. Deco frog, pottery, ca. 1935, US, 2¾"h; D; $200.00 – 225.00.

Plate 643. Begging frog, majolica, ca. 1920, European, 3⅝"h; D; $200.00 – 225.00.

Plate 644. Jumping frog, pottery, ca. 1925, US, 2¼"h; C; $100.00 – 125.00.

Plate 645. Hole-eyed frog, pottery, ca. 1910, could be related to hole-eyed pigs (Austrian-Czech), 2¼"h; C; $100.00 – 125.00.

Plate 646. Toad, pottery with lusterware glaze, ca. 1920, US, 2⅞"h; as shown coin slot will not accommodate even a dime; D; $175.00 – 200.00.

Plate 647. California bear, pottery, ca. 1890, US, 3⅛"h; "Hogan's" stamped in bottom; resembles California Bear Flag Republic bear (1848); E; $350.00 – 450.00.

Plate 648. Polar bear, same as #101 except with lusterware glaze, 2½"h; comes in a several sizes and finishes; A; $35.00 – 50.00.

Plate 649. Panda bear walking, same as #101 except 2½"h; comes in several sizes, poses, and finishes, two shown; A; $35.00 – 50.00.

Plate 650. Panda bear sitting, same as #101 except overpaint, 4⅜"h.

Plate 651. Walking bear, pottery, ca. 1920, US; C; $100.00 – 125.00.

Plate 652. Stretching bear, same as #144 except porcelain, colored version, 3"h; C; $125.00 – 150.00.

Plate 653. Souvenir Bear, pottery, ca. 1920, US(?); C; $125.00 – 150.00.

Plate 654. Grizzly bear, pottery, ca. 1930, US, 6⅜"h; D; $200.00 – 250.00.

Plate 655. Fat bear, pottery, ca. 1920, US(?); D; $175.00 – 200.00.

Plate 656. Teddy bear, pottery, ca. 1930, US, Cambridge Art Pottery(?), 4½"h; C; $125.00 – 150.00.

Plate 657. Stuffed bear, pottery, ca. 1940 US, Rio Hondo(?); C; $100.00 – 125.00.

Plate 634. Small beehive, same as #273 except 2½"h; like #633 has round hole for cork; D; $250.00 – 300.00.

Plate 635. Beehive with mouse, same as #144, colored version, 3"h; Austria on strip; D; $225.00 – 250.00.

Plate 636. Mice in bun, pottery, ca. 1925, European(?); D; $200.00 – 225.00.

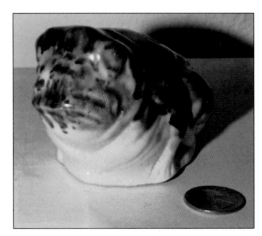

Plate 637. Frog's head, same #54 except C; $125.00 – 150.00.

Plate 638. Frog, same as #273 except 2⅞"h; C; $225.00 – 250.00.

Plate 639. Sitting frog, same as #273 except 2¾"h; C; $225.00 – 250.00.

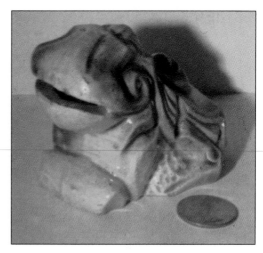

Plate 640. Comic frog, same as #101 except overpaint, comes in several sizes starting at 3⅞"h; B; $75.00 – 100.00.

Plate 641. Frog with ribbon, porcelain(?), ca. 1925, European; C; $150.00 – 175.00.

Plate 642. Deco frog, pottery, ca. 1935, US, 2¾"h; D; $200.00 – 225.00.

Plate 643. Begging frog, majolica, ca. 1920, European, 3⅝"h; D; $200.00 – 225.00.

Plate 644. Jumping frog, pottery, ca. 1925, US, 2¼"h; C; $100.00 – 125.00.

Plate 645. Hole-eyed frog, pottery, ca. 1910, could be related to hole-eyed pigs (Austrian-Czech), 2¼"h; C; $100.00 – 125.00.

Plate 658. Bear with limb, same as #144 except 3⅞"h; C; $135.00 – 160.00.

Plate 659. White bear with limb, porcelain, ca. 1925, Germany(?); D; $225.00 – 275.00.

Plate 660. Bear with money bag, stoneware, ca. 1900, US, 6"h; D; $200.00 – 225.00.

Plate 661. Bear with shamrock, same as #54 except 4¼"h; comes in smaller size, also C; C; $150.00 – 175.00.

Plate 662. Bear with baby bear, same as #144 except colored, 4¾"h; C; $150.00 – 175.00.

Plate 663. Bear with locked honey pot, same as #144 except 2¾"h; B; $75.00 – 120.00.

Plate 664. Bear with trunk, same as #557 except C; $100.00 – 125.00.

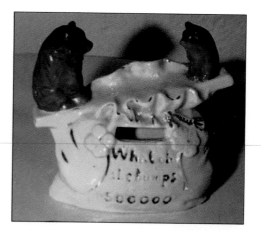

Plate 665. Bears on money bag, same as #576 except 3¼"; B; $75.00 – 100.00.

Plate 666. Bear with plate, pottery with overpaint, ca. 1910, US, 5"h; E; $300.00 – 325.00.

Plate 667. Two Upright Little Bears, pottery, ca. 1920, US, 4¾"h; B; $85.00 – 110.00.

Plate 668. Bear on books, same as #394 except bisque, 4¼"h; C; $100.00 – 150.00.

Plate 669. Tiny fish, pottery, ca. 1900, US(?), 1⅞"h; D; $250.00 – 275.00.

Plate 670. Big fish, redware, ca. 1870, US, 3⅜"h; F; $450.00 – 550.00.

Plate 671. Fish with slot in head, pottery, ca. 1900, US; D; $250.00 – 275.00.

Plate 672. Fish with dorsal slot, same as #54(?) except 2⅝"h; C; $125.00 – 150.00.

Plate 673. Luster fish, porcelain with lusterware glaze, ca. 1925, European(?), 2⅛"h; C; $140.00 – 180.00.

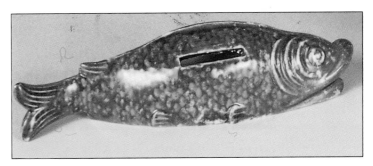

Plate 674. Fish with slot in side, pottery, ca. 1915, US(?); B; $75.00 – 125.00.

Plate 675. Comic fish, same as #101 except 3⅝"h; B; $85.00 – 100.00.

Plate 676. Narrow comic fish, same as #101 except 4⅛"h; C; $100.00 – 150.00.

Plate 677. Big mouth fish, same as #101 except Occupied Japan, ca. 1950; B; $100.00 – 125.00.

Plate 678. Ribbed fish, pottery, ca. 1935, US, 3⅝"h; C; $100.00 – 125.00.

Plate 679. Tiny monkey's head, porcelain bisque, ca. 1925, German(?), 2¼"h; D; $175.00 – 200.00.

Plate 680. Talking monkey's head, same as #54(?); D; $225.00 – 250.00.

Plate 681. Smiling monkey, same as #54 except 3⅜"h; C; $125.00 – 150.00.

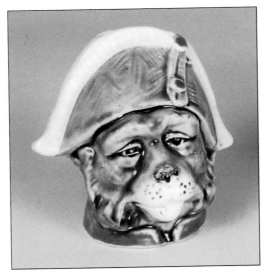

Plate 682. Monkey with fancy hat, same as #2 except D; $250.00 – 300.00.

Plate 683. Monkey with stick, pottery, ca. 1900, England(?), Rockingham; C; $135.00 – 160.00.

Plate 684. Monkey with top hat, pottery(?), ca. 1920, Europe(?), 3⅞"h; D; $225.00 – 250.00.

Plate 685. Resting monkey, same as #144 except 3⅝"h; B; $100.00 – 125.00.

Plate 686. Monkey on rock, same as #144 except 4¾"h; AUSTRIA raised strip on rear; D; $225.00 – 250.00.

Plate 687. Monkey swatting fly, same as #101 except 4½"h; C; $100.00 – 125.00.

Plate 688. Monkey eating fruit, same as #273 except 4⅞"h; C; $200.00 – 275.00.

Plate 689. Monkey holding sack, same as #54 except 4¼"h; B; $85.00 – 110.00.

Plate 690. Monkey holding pear, porcelain, ca. 1935, European(?), 6"h; a Mottaheddh Design on paper label on bottom; C; $125.00 – 150.00.

Plate 691. Monkey with large coconut, pottery, ca. 1910, US, Cambridge Art Pottery, Cambridge, Ohio, 5⅛"h; C; $200.00 – 250.00.

Plate 692. Monkey hugging money bag, porcelain, ca. 1925, Germany; B; $85.00 – 110.00.

Plate 693. Monkey on orange, pottery, ca. 1920, Mexico(?), 5⅜"h; E; $275.00 – 325.00.

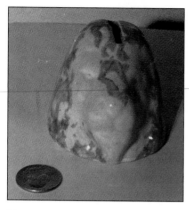

Plate 694. Lion's head, same as #273 except 2½"h; D; $250.00 – 350.00.

Plate 695. Reclining lion, same as #144 3⅜"h; D; $250.00 – 300.00. Tan monochrome, same size known (also smaller tan version); C; $175.00 – 200.00.

Plate 696. Art deco lion, pottery, ca. 1935, US, 2¾"h; D; $200.00 – 250.00.

Plate 697. Stylized lion, low fired pottery, ca. 1925, Mexico; C; $135.00 – 160.00.

Plate 698. Camel resting, same as #144 except colored versions 3¼"h and 3⅜"h; "1908" handwritten on bottom; C; $150.00 – 175.00.

Plate 699. Comic camel, pottery, ca. 1940, US, 4⅝"h; B; $85.00 – 110.00.

Plate 700. Camel with howdah, same as #144(?) colored version; C; $200.00 – 225.00.

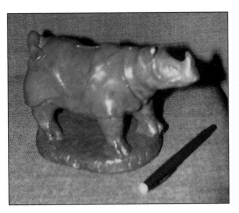

Plate 701. Rhino, pottery, ca. 1825, US, Pennsylvania, 4⅞"h (described and priced by Sidney Gecker); F; $3,200.00 – 3,500.00.

Plate 702. Hippopotamus, same as #144 except 2½"h; D; $225.00 – 250.00.

Plate 703. Fox with glasses, pottery, ca. 1890, US, 3"h; C; $150.00 – 200.00.

Plate 704. Fox on rock base, same as #144 except colored, 3½"h; Austria on raised strip; D; $200.00 – 250.00.

Plate 705. Fox, pottery, ca. 1880 England, Rockingham, 3⅝"h; E; $450.00 – 500.00.

Plate 706. Serval cat, same as #144 two monochrome sizes 4⅛"h and 5⅝"h; C; $150.00 – 200.00; and D; $275.00 – 325.00.

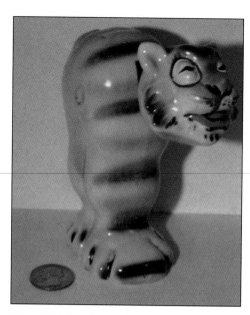

Plate 707. Mechanical tiger, same as #294.

Plate 708. Possum in wheelchair, same as #54(?) except C; $150.00 – 200.00.

Plate 709. Possum standing, pottery, ca. 1900, US, 5½"h; C; $135.00 – 160.00.

Plate 710. Skunk (probably Walt Disney's Flower from *Bambi*), pottery, ca. 1940, US, 3⅜"h; E; $300.00+.

Plate 711. Sloth(?), same as #54 except 3⅝"h; D; $200.00 – 225.00.

Plate 712. Decorated turtle, pottery, ca. 1900, US(?), 2¼"h; D; $200.00 – 250.00.

Plate 713. Plain turtle, pottery, ca. 1890, Rockingham(?), 2¼"h; C; $150.00 – 175.00.

Plate 714. Sea turtle, same as #144 except 2⅛"h; C; $150.00 – 175.00.

Plate 715. Sea lion, same as #144 except D; Austria on raised strip; $200.00 – 225.00.

Plate 716. Cricket, same as #144 except two colored sizes, 2"h and 2¼"h; D; $225.00 – 250.00.

Plate 717. Lobster lying down, porcelain, ca. 1925, Germany, 1¾"h; 5028 incised on bottom; C; $125.00 – 175.00.

Plate 718. Lobster sitting up, same as #717 except 3⅛"h; 5047 incised on bottom.

Plate 719. Lobster at poke, porcelain, ca. 1925, Germany, Shafer and Vater(?), 2½"h; C; $150.00 – 175.00.

Plate 720. Alligator(?) emerging from egg, pottery, ca. 1910, US(?); D; $250.00 – 300.00.

Plate 721. Snail, possibly same as #191 except D; $250.00 – 300.00.

Plate 722. Sea snail(?), pottery, ca. 1925, European(?); D; $250.00 – 300.00.

Plate 723. Snail covered globes, redware, ca. 1860, England, Sussexware, 9⅝"h; "1863 M.M." slip decorated; E; $450.00 – 550.00.

Plate 724. Conch shell, porcelain lusterware finish, ca. 1930, European(?), 4"h; D; $350.00 – 400.00.

Plate 725. Tiny house, pottery, ca. 1850, England, Staffordshire, 3¾"h; D; note the primitive irregular features in early Staffordshire pottery; because Staffordshire is collected by a variety of collectors it is generally priced higher than other pieces of similar rarity; $300.00 – 400.00.

Plate 726. Toll house, same as #725 except ca. 1860, 3⅞"h; C; $225.00 – 275.00.

Plate 727. Small cottage, same as #725 except coleslaw appears, ca. 1870, 3¼"h; usual salmon color, C; $175.00 – 200.00; white color variation; D; $275.00 – 325.00.

Plate 728. Two-story house, same as #725 except ca. 1880, 3⅞"h; C; $225.00 – 300.00.

Plate 729. Fancy cottage, same as #725 except ca. 1900, 4⅝"h; "Staffordshire Ware, England," ink stamped on bottom with knotted rope symbol; B; $175.00 – 200.00.

Plate 730. Three-story house, same as #725 except ca. 1900, 6⅜"h; C; $275.00 – 350.00.

Plate 731. Plain cottage, same as #725 except ca. 1915, 4⅜"h; B; $150.00 – 200.00.

Plate 732. One chimney cottage, same as #725 except ca. 1915, 4½"h; C; many money boxes were also designed as pastille burners and when adapted for money boxes the chimneys were left as is, as in this example; $200.00 – 225.00.

Plate 733. Flowered lawn cottage, same as #725 except ca. 1920 – 30(?), 3¾"h; B; $125.00 – 150.00.

Plate 734. Bank bank, same as #725 except ca. 1920(?), 4¾"h; B; $125.00 – 150.00.

Plate 735. Castle entrance, same as #725 except ca. 1890; D; $350.00 – 400.00.

Plate 736. Elaborate two-story house, pottery, ca. 1850, US, Greenwood Pottery, 5½"h; "Fritz Knopp" written in faded gold along lower front edge; these are often mistaken for Staffordshire, but early Greenwood usually had names, initials, or dates on lower edge and were white; greenwood Pottery ceased operations in 1857; after their demise some pottery or potteries began a replica of their design sans names, initials and/or dates (see 737); D; $350.00 – 400.00.

Plate 737. Greenwood replica, pottery, ca. 1920 – 1930(?), England/US(?), 5"h; B; $100.00 – 125.00.

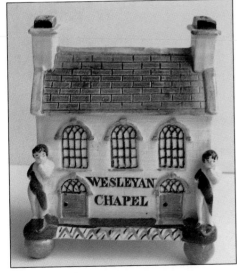

Plate 738. Wesleyan Chapel (aka Pratt Cottages, see text), pottery, ca. 1845, England, Staffordshire, 6"h (approx); these were given to children for regular attendance at Sunday School, the larger and more elaborate for longer, better attendance; they often had their names inscribed (see 739); note Bun Feet; E; $2,300.00 – 3,000.00.

Plate 739. Bridge St. Academy (aka Pratt Cottages, see text and 740), same as #738 except 4⅞"h; Mr. Maltby was recipient; E; $1,500.00 – 1,900.00.

Plate 740. Pratt Cottage, same as #738 except 4¾"h; note people peering out of upper windows; D; $700.00 – 1,000.00.

Plate 741. Shakespeare Savings Bank, same as #725 except ca. 1930(?), 4½"h; B; $100.00 – 150.00.

Plate 742. "Ann Hathaway's Cottage" (on lower front edge), same as #725 except ca. 1920(?), 4⅝"h; C; $250.00 – 300.00.

Plate 743. Burns Cottage, pottery, ca. 1920, Scotland, 2¾"h; D; $300.00 – 350.00.

Plate 744. General Grant's Log Cabin, same as #144 except 2½"h; backside shown; C; $200.00 – 250.00.

Plate 745. Ancestral home of President McKinley in Co. Antrim, Ireland, porcelain (possibly belleek), ca. 1930, Ireland, 3¼"h; E; $500.00 – 600.00.

Plate 746. Lincoln cabin, same as #144 except 2¾"h; Van Dyke Tea advertising gift; A; $25.00 – 40.00.

Plate 747. Six-sided building, stoneware, ca. 1920, unknown, 4⅜"h; probably a replica of an early building, currently a mystery; C; $175.00 – 200.00.

Plate 748. Turret Building, pottery, ca. 1900, European(?), 4¾"h; slot on bottom, may be adapted pastille burner; D; $250.00 – 275.00.

Plate 749. Early house, same as #725 except ca. 1895, 4¾"h; D; $175.00 – 225.00.

Plate 750. House, same as #725 except ca. 1850, 5"h; D; $275.00 – 300.00.

Plate 751. Norges Bank, pottery, ca. 1920(?), Norweign(?), 2¼"; C; $150.00 – 175.00.

Plate 752. Block cabin, pottery, ca. 1900, US, 3⅜"h; usually found in the northeast; C; $150.00 – 200.00.

Plate 753. Two-story block building, pottery, ca. 1880, US(?); note one chimney broken off; D; $225.00 – 275.00.

Plate 754. Tiny chapel, pottery, ca. 1880, England(?), Rockingham; C; $175.00 – 225.00.

Plate 755. Three-story home, pottery, ca. 1795, England, stamped "C. Wally's Ware," 4¼"h (one of very few verified eighteenth century banks); E; $500.00 – 700.00.

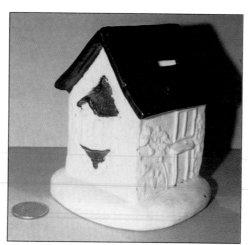

Plate 756. House with mansard roof, pottery, ca. 1900, England, 4⅛"h; several colors; B; $100.00 – 125.00.

Plate 757. Decorated cottage, pottery bisque with cobalt glazed roofs, ca. 1910, England, 4¾"h; E; $450.00 – 550.00.

Plate 758. Man, dog, and cottage, porcelain, ca. 1910, England(?), 3¼"h; note man with three legs to indicate walking; E; $400.00 – 550.00.

Plate 759. Thatched cottage, pottery, ca. 1920, England(?), 3⅞"h; D; $200.00 – 225.00.

Plate 760. Cottage with stone chimney, pottery, ca. 1930, European, "Josef Steidl, Znaim" on bottom, 4"h; C; $175.00 – 200.00.

Plate 761. Cottage with shrubs, pottery, ca. 1930, US(?); C; $150.00 – 175.00.

Plate 762. Primitive cottage, same as #191(?) except 3⅞"h; C; $200.00 – 225.00.

Plate 763. Tiny house, porcelain bisque, ca. 1920, German(?), 2¼"h; C; $150.00 – 175.00.

Plate 764. Tiled roof house, same as #101 except 3⅜"h; note similarity to Pratt Cottages; C; $100.00 – 150.00.

Plate 765. Dutch house, majolica, Delft, ca. 1920, Netherlands, 3⅜"h; C; $150.00 – 200.00.

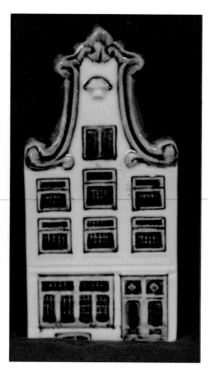

Plate 766. Canal house, same as #765.

Plate 767. T. Pothuis house, same as #765 except ca. 1930, 4⅞"h; "Spaarbank Voor De Stad Amsterdam" under the glaze on back. Metal KLT on back; C; $150.00 – 175.00.

Plate 768. Two gabled roof house, porcelain, ca. 1900, European, 3"h; C; $125.00 – 150.00.

Plate 769. Oriental house, same as #144, 3⅛"h; D; $175.00 – 200.00.

Plate 770. Two-story simple house, pottery, ca. 1940, US, 3"h; "Louis Hann and Son, 1939" incised on bottom; C; $125.00 – 150.00.

Plate 771. Bank building, same as #54 except 3⅜"h; some variations and other sizes known; B; $90.00 – 120.00.

Plate 772. Souvenir building, porcelain, ca. 1925, Germany, 2⅝"h; Fresno County Courthouse, Fresno, California, pictured; D; $200.00 – 225.00.

Plate 773. Stone church, redware, ca. 1890, US(?), 3⅜"h; D; $200.00 – 225.00.

Plate 774. Clapboard church, pottery, ca. 1940, US, 3¼"h; has oblong hole cast in bottom; B; $75.00 – 85.00.

Plate 775. Chickens at house, porcelain, ca. 1930, Germany; C; $150.00 – 175.00.

Plate 776. The Williamsburgh Savings Bank, Central Tower, Tower of Strength, pottery, 1940 and later, US, McCoy Pottery, 4¼"h; several McCoys of this vintage exist and all are A's; A; $20.00 – 30.00.

Vegetables, Fruits & Edibles

Plate 777. Acorn, pottery, ca. 1900, US, 3⅝"h; C; $100.00 – 125.00.

Plate 778. Acorn, same as #54(?) except 2⅞"h; inscribed around top: "Acorn Stoves Will Save Half Your Fuel Money"; B; $85.00 – 110.00. Also without advertising rated C; $125.00 – 150.00.

Plate 779. Stylized acorn, stoneware, ca. 1910, US(?), 4¾"h; comes in other sizes and colors; D; $200.00 – 225.00.

Plate 780. Sunflower blossom, pottery, ca. 1920, US, reported as Weller(?), 1¼"h; D; $225.00 – 250.00.

Plate 781. Bell pepper, redware, ca. 1920, US, 2⅝"h; C; $150.00 – 175.00.

Plate 782. Ripening tomato, pottery, ca. 1920, US, 3¼"h; D; $200.00 – 225.00.

Plate 783. Eating corn, pottery, ca. 1900, US, 3"h; D; $200.00 – 225.00.

Plate 784. Corn on cob, pottery, ca. 1925, Mexico; C; $125.00 – 150.00.

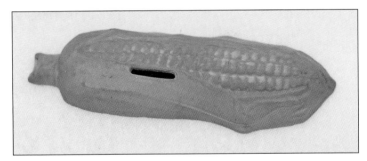

Plate 785. Corn from stalk, pottery, ca. 1920, US(?); C; $150.00 – 175.00.

Plate 786. Orange, redware, ca. 1890, US, Roseville(?), 3"h; D; $175.00 – 200.00.

Plate 787. Green apple, redware, ca. 1890, US, Roseville(?), 3"h; C; $150.00 – 175.00.

Plate 788. Red apple, pottery, ca. 1900, US, 2⅝"h; C; $125.00 – 150.00.

Plate 789. Avacado, pottery, ca. 1920, Mexican(?), 2"h; C; $150.00 – 175.00.

Plate 790. Pear, pottery, ca. 1850, US, 3"h; D; $200.00 – 250.00.

Plate 791. Flowered pear, majolica, ca. 1930, European(?), 4¼"h; C; $100.00 – 125.00.

Plate 792. Pear with birds, pottery, ca. 1920, US(?); D; $150.00 – 175.00.

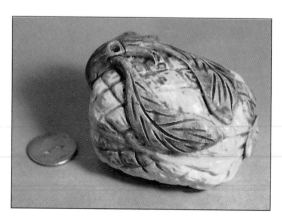

Plate 793. Pineapple with leaves, pottery, ca. 1910, US, 2⅜"h; D; $175.00 – 200.00.

Plate 794. Pineapple, same as #101 except Occupied Japan, ca. 1950, 2½"h.

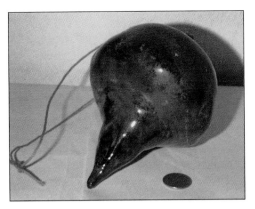

Plate 795. Gourd, pottery, ca. 1920, Mexico(?), 4½"h; D; $150.00 – 175.00.

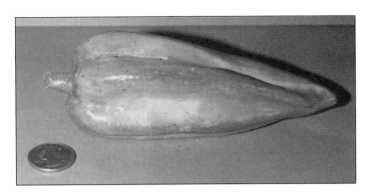

Plate 796. Chili pepper, pottery, ca. 1920, Mexico, 2⅛"h; B; $75.00 – 100.00.

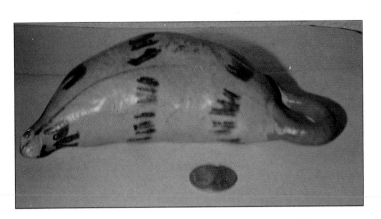

Plate 797. Banana, same as #796 except 2⅜"h.

Plate 798. Melon, same as #796 except 2⅞"h; marked "Made In Mexico."

Plate 799. Rough melon, pottery, ca. 1910, US, 3⅛"h; C; $125.00 – 150.00.

Plate 800. Pumpkin, pottery, ca. 1920, US, 3⅝"h; other colors; C; $150.00 – 175.00.

Plate 801. Pumpkin with leaves, pottery, ca. 1910, US, 2¼"h; C; $150.00 – 175.00.

Plate 802. Egg, redware, ca. 1880, US, 1⅝"h; decorated and inscribed "Jinny"; E; $275.00 – 300.00.

Plate 803. Basket of fruit, redware, ca. 1900, Mexico(?), 3¾"h; several tropical fruits noted; E; $250.00 – 300.00.

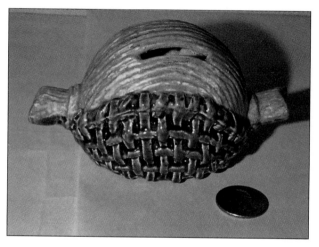

Plate 804. Fruit bowl, pottery, ca. 1890, US(?); D; $175.00 – 200.00.

Plate 805. Tamale, pottery, ca. 1930, US(?), 2¾"h; D; $175.00 – 200.00.

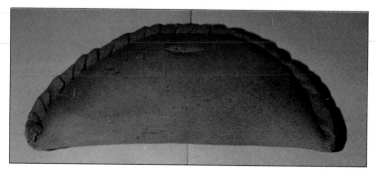

Plate 806. Turnover, pottery, ca. 1920, US(?), 1½"h; D; $150.00 – 175.00.

Pots, Jugs, Globes
& Other Simple Forms

Most early coin banks follow simple pot, jug, globe, and round style. Those with various decorations, dates, and writing hold our attention. The many flowered examples were reportedly done by women and children during winter evenings for later gift giving. Only a representative number are shown to cover the broadest spectrum possible. Many of these jugs were made in great quantities.

Plate 807. Oldest bank, terra cotta (redware), ca. 100AD, Roman, 4"h (approx), F; no price. Collectors often attribute the oldest bank and oldest ceramic bank to the temple-shaped treasure house dating to 100 – 200BC. I disagree. It has an open back unlike any other coin bank until the 1930s. It looks like an incense burner and works like one. I think the so-called coin slot in front is merely the vent for the incense. It was found with a few coins in it which I think were hidden there. A number of reproductions of it exist. Bank #807 was found in the catacombs of Rome and is accuratly dated, it competes with several other banks of that period including one bronze. #807 is exhibited in the Vatican's Museo Sacro Salva Danerio Armateo (Savings Bank Cabinet) #18, it has palm decorations on the front. Other early banks are seen in *Die Kultur der Sparsamkeit*, Hans Peter Thurn.

Plate 808. Globular with finial, pottery, ca. 1550, English, approx. 3½"h; resides in City Museum and Art Gallery, Stoke On Trent, Staffordshire, England; servants and craftspeople of this period kept banks like this prominently displayed to receive gratuities from clients; they were broken open at Christmas; F; no price.

Plate 810. Handleless jug with horizontal slot, light clay pottery, ca. 1840, US, 4"h; A; $35.00 – 60.00.

Plate 811. Jug with horizontal slot, redware with light glaze, ca. 1850, US, 4⅜"h; A; $50.00 – 75.00.

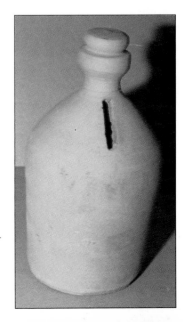

Plate 809. Handleless jug with vertical slot, redware, ca. 1840, US, 4¾"h; B; $50.00 – 100.00.

Plate 812. Gobular urn with finial, pottery, ca. 1850, US, 4⅛"h; 122 incised on front, unknown reason; C; $110.00 – 135.00.

Plate 813. American Legion jug, pottery, ca. 1925, US, 4¾"h; paper label on back says, "Give A Cent A Day Your Dues I Will Pay — Wilbur M. Comeau Post #4"; C; $175.00 – 200.00.

Plate 814. Globe urn with tall finial, pottery, ca. 1900, US, 4⅛"h; "God loveth a cheerful giver"; C; $150.00 – 175.00.

Plate 816. Globe urn with angular slot, pottery, ca. 1850, US, 3⅞"h; C; $125.00 – 150.00.

Plate 815. Globe urn with decorated neck and vertical slot, pottery light black glaze, ca. 1850, US, 3¾"h; C; $150.00 – 175.00.

Plate 817. Jug with high handle, low fired redware with black glaze, ca. 1790(?), US, 4¾"h; D; $250.00 – 300.00.

Plate 818. Jug with fancy stopper, stoneware, ca. 1880, US, 5¼"h; D; $200.00 – 250.00.

Plate 819. Jug with mottled glaze, redware, ca. 1860, US; D; $200.00 – 250.00.

Plate 820. W. Smith urn banks, redware with spattered slip glaze, ca. 1890, US, Pennsylvania, 4"h; collection of Lester Breininger; D; $1,000.00 – 1,500.00.

Plate 823. "From Cottage City" jug, pottery run glaze, ca. 1900, US, 4¼"h; C; $140.00 – 180.00.

Plate 821. Spattered glaze globe urn with finial, redware, ca. 1890, US, 5⅞"h; D; $500.00 – 700.00.

Plate 822. Flowered jug "I Need The Money — Jamestown Expo 1907," pottery, ca. 1905, US; C; $140.00 – 180.00.

Plate 824. Flowered jug, redware with black glaze, ca. 1860, US, 4¾"h; C; $120.00 – 150.00.

Plate 825. "Birthday Offerings W.C.T.U." (Women's Christian Temperance Union), redware, ca. 1910, US, 4⅝"h; D; $175.00 – 200.00.

Plate 826. A.Y.P. Expo 1909 — "I Need The Money," pottery, 1907, US, 3⅝"h; C; $120.00 – 140.00.

Plate 827. Motto jug, redware, ca. 1890, US, 4⅜"h; inscribed "Let us to do good therefore as we have opportunity"; D; $175.00 – 200.00.

Plate 828. Fancy jug, pottery, ca. 1920, US; C; $150.00 – 175.00.

Plate 829. Drip glaze flowered urn, pottery, ca. 1900, US, 4½"h; C; $140.00 – 180.00.

Plate 830. Urn with appliqués, pottery, ca. 1880, US, 4"h; D; $175.00 – 200.00.

Plate 831. Urn with forget me nots, redware with black glaze, ca. 1890, US, 4¼"h; C; $125.00 – 150.00.

Plate 832. "Francis C. Taylor" globe urn, stoneware with black glaze, ca. 1820, US, "Barton Pottery, Parque Isle, Pa." (on front); E; $350.00 – 500.00.

Plate 833. Ornate globe urn, majolica(?), ca. 1920, European(?), 4⅛"h; D; $200.00 – 250.00.

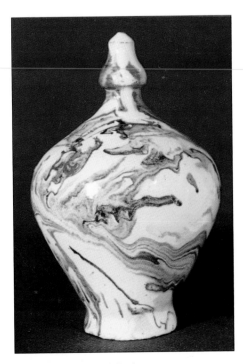

Plate 834. Scroddled urn, pottery, ca. 1900, US; D; $175.00 – 200.00.

Plate 835. Pointed finial urn, stoneware, ca. 1880, US, 5⅛"h; B; $125.00 – 150.00.

Plate 836. Globe with dot decoration, pottery, ca. 1900, European, 2⅝"h; C; $125.00 – 160.00.

Plate 837. "Love" decorated urn, stoneware, ca. 1880, US, 3¼"h; D; $150.00 – 200.00.

Plate 838. "Jas Honye, De 8, 1796," redware with sgraffitto decoration, 1796, England, Devonshire(?), 2½"h; collection Lester Breininger; F; $750.00 – 1,000.00.

Plate 839. "Columbian Exposition, Chicago, Ill 1893" globe, pottery, ca. 1893, US, two sizes; D; $400.00 – 600.00.

Plate 840. Covered dish with tall finial, pottery, ca. 1900, US, Biloxi, Mississippi, George Ohr, 4½"h; F; $550.00 – 700.00.

Plate 841. "F. Tapper, 1859" urn, pottery, 1859, England, 5¾"h; these come with and without names and dates, of a number available only this and #842 are shown; D; $200.00 – 250.00.

Plate 842. "Hedley, 1912," ornate globe, same as #841 except more ornate, later date, and 7¾"h.

Plate 843. "WILL. M SWIND-HILL, 1850," monument, urn, pottery, ca. 1850, England; D; $200.00 – 250.00.

Plate 844. "Hanna Watts, 1846," pottery, 1846, England(?); note soldiers in freize; E; $350.00 – 450.00.

Plate 845. "J. METCALF SURGEY, BORN MAY 10, 1885," coat of arms, stoneware, ca. 1885, England, 4¾"h; finial broken off; D; $200.00 – 250.00.

Plate 846. "S.H.B., 1854" in slip, redware, 1854, US, 4¾"h; E; $400.00 – 500.00.

Plate 847. "Martha Johnson, Born Feby 25th, 1850," pottery, 1850, England, 5¼"h; D; $250.00 – 300.00.

Plate 848. Delft urn, majolica delftware, ca. 1900, Netherlands, 8¼"h; D; $250.00 – 300.00.

Plate 849. Medicine bottle, pottery, ca. 1920, US, 4⅜"h; B; $100.00 – 125.00.

Plate 850. Pot with small neck, stoneware, ca. 1850, US, 4⅛"h; E; $200.00 – 250.00.

Plate 851. Pot with large neck, redware, ca. 1850, US; C; $90.00 – 110.00.

Plate 852. Teepee-shaped jug, stoneware, ca. 1920, US, 4¾"h; "Thirsty? Kentucky moonshine"; D; $175.00 – 200.00.

Plate 853. Chaos dish, pottery (beautiful glaze), ca. 1925, US; E; $250.00 – 300.00.

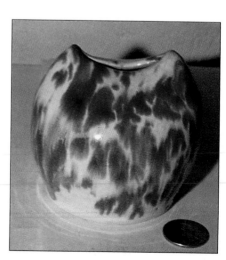

Plate 854. Twin peaked pot, pottery, ca. 1925, US(?), 3¼"h; C; $100.00 – 125.00.

Plate 855. Tall bottle, pottery, ca. 1910, European(?), 7½"h; D; $175.00 – 200.00.

Plate 856. Triple globe, pottery, ca. 1850, England, Sussexware; E; $300.00 – 350.00.

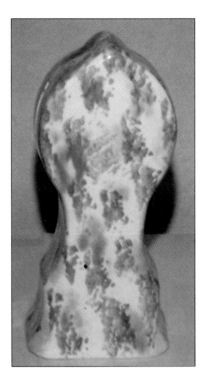

Plate 857. Clock-shaped bank, pottery, ca. 1915, US, 7⅛"h; D; $175.00 – 200.00.

Plate 858. Ohr Barrel, pottery, ca. 1900 US, Biloxi, Miss., George E. Ohr, 3⅞"h; F; $500.00 – 600.00.

Plate 859. Keg, pottery, ca. 1850, US, 4½"h (priced by Sidney Gecker); E; $600.00 – 800.00.

Plate 860. Man in barrel, pottery, ca. 1900, US, 3⅝"h; C; $175.00 – 200.00. "For Health, Martinsville, Ind. 1904" on front. Others known without inscriptions; B; $125.00 – 150.00.

Plate 861. Souvenir barrel, porcelain, ca. 1920, Germany, 3"h; C; $150.00 – $175.00.

Plate 862. Irregular barrel, stoneware with drip glaze, ca. 1910, US, 2⅜"h; E; $250.00 – 275.00.

Plate 863. Plain barrel, same as #54 except 2¾"h; B; $75.00 – 100.00.

Plate 864. Colored barrel, pottery, ca. 1930(?), Portugal, 2⅝"h; may be modern; C; $75.00 – 100.00.

Plate 865. Wood grained barrel, same as #54 except 3⅛"h; 1483 incised on bottom; C; $100.00 – 125.00.

Plate 866. Gold band barrel, redware, ca. 1870, US, 3¾"h; A; $50.00 – 75.00.

Plate 867. Barrel barrel, same as #54(?) except 2⅞"h; B; $75.00 – 85.00.

Plate 868. Shoe with laces, pottery, ca. 1900, England, 2⅜"h (a nearly identical shoe is exhibited in the Fitzwilliam Museum, Cambridge, England); C; $150.00 – 175.00.

Plate 869. Dutch shoe, pottery, ca. 1900, Netherlands, 2"h; C; $100.00 – 125.00.

Plate 870. High button shoe with gusset, pottery, ca. 1890, US(?), 3¼"h; C; $125.00 – 150.00.

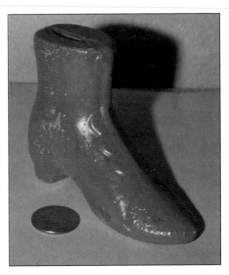

Plate 871. High button shoe, crude pottery, ca. 1890, US, 3⅛"h; D; $150.00 – 175.00.

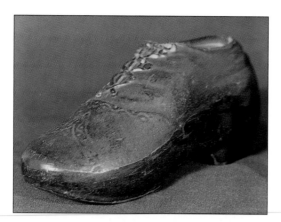

Plate 872. Klunky shoe, redware, ca. 1910, US; D; $150.00 – 175.00.

Plate 873. Shoe with spats, pottery, ca. 1920, Swiss, 3⅛"h; E; $200.00 – 250.00.

Plate 874. Tall shoe, same as #101 except 3¼"h; B; $75.00 – 100.00.

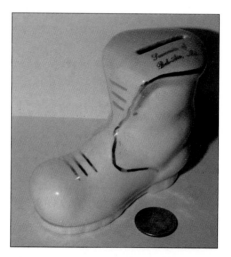

Plate 875. Child's boot, pottery, ca. 1940, US, 4"h; A; $30.00 – 40.00.

Plate 876. Shoe with mouse and cat, same as #101 except 2½"h; has Mt. Fuji symbol on bottom; B; $75.00 – 85.00.

Vehicles & Ships

Plate 877. Beach wagon, Delftware (majolica), ca. 1920, Netherlands, 4¾"h; E; $325.00 – 400.00.

Plate 878. Gypsy wagon, porcelain, ca. 1925, Czech, 3½"h; crown over shield symbol with Genma angled across shield on bottom; C; $150.00 – 175.00.

Plate 879. Fancy horse coach, pottery, ca. 1915, Mexico(?), 3¼"h; D; $150.00 – 225.00.

Plate 880. Covered wagon, redware, ca. 1850, US, Pennsylvania, 6"h (priced by Sidney Gecker); F; $1,000.00 – 1,200.00.

Plate 881. Trolley, pottery, ca. 1915, US, 3"h; C; $150.00 – 175.00.

Plate 882. Cable car, pottery, ca. 1940, US, San Francisco, 4½"h; B; $75.00 – 100.00.

Plate 883. Train engine, same as #144 except porcelain two sizes, 2⅞"h (shown) and 3½"h; B; $85.00 – 110.00; and C; $125.00 – 150.00.

Plate 884. Auto, pottery with lusterware drip glaze, ca. 1935, US, 2⅛"h; D; $200.00 – 250.00.

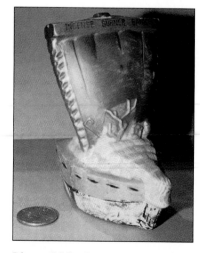

Plate 885. Japanese Fortune Ship, same as #101 except 4⅜"h; "Incense Burner, Bank" written across top of mast and serves both uses; C; $100.00 – 150.00.

Plate 886. Ark, same as #54 except 3½"h; C; $125.00 – 150.00.

Plate 887. Battleship, same as #144 3½"h; D; $200.00 – 225.00.

Plate 888. Tank bank, pottery, ca. 1915, England, 3¼"h; C; $150.00 – 175.00.

Plate 889. House trailer, pottery, ca. 1935, England, 3⅜"h; C; $125.00 – 150.00.

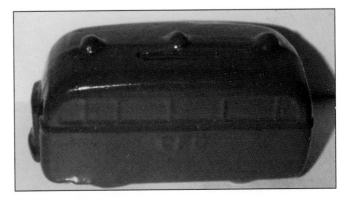

Plate 890. Mobile trailer, pottery, ca. 1935, European, 3⅝"h; CFD on side; D; $150.00 – 175.00.

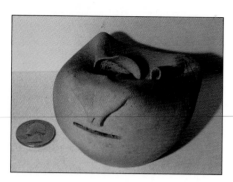

Plate 891. Double prepuce, pottery, ca. 1900, US, Biloxi, Miss, George E. Ohr, 2½"h; piece as described by dealer based on Ohr's sexual bent; F; $500.00 – 700.00.

Plate 892. Flowered top, same as #891.

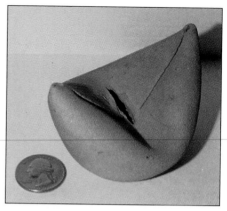

Plate 893. Folded top, same as #891 except 2⅛"h.

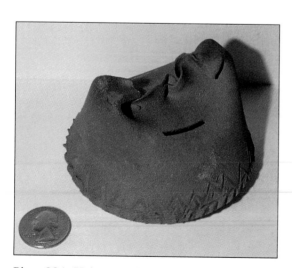

Plate 894. Vulva opening, same as #891 except 2¼"h.

Plate 895. Folded top, similar to George Ohr #891, glazed pottery, ca. 1900(?), US; F; $200.00 – 1,000.00(?).

Plate 896. Vase, pottery with flint, enamel-like glaze, ca. 1930, US(?), 5¼"h; D; $125.00 – 175.00.

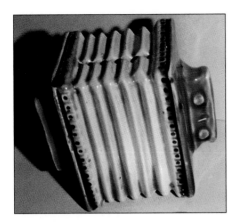

Plate 897. Concertina, majolica, ca. 1925, European(?); C; $150.00 – 200.00.

Plate 898. Creel, pottery, ca. 1930, US, 2⅜"h; D; $175.00 – 200.00.

Plate 899. Tomb, pottery, ca. 1920, Danish(?), 2⅜"h; "For Heller and Kronen" on other side; D; $225.00 – 250.00.

Plate 900. Mounted cannon, pottery, ca. 1900, US(?), 3½"h; D; $225.00 – 250.00.

Plate 901. Pistol, pottery, ca. 1910, US(?), 1⅞"h; C; $175.00 – 200.00.

Plate 902. Irish hat, same as #54 except D; $175.00 – 200.00.

Plate 903. Baseball, pottery, ca. 1910, US, 2¾"h; E; $250.00 – 350.00.

Plate 904. Ball with Christmas tree, pottery, ca. 1920, US(?), 2¼"h; D; $200.00 – 250.00.

Plate 905. World globe with motto, pottery, ca. 1940 – 50(?), US, 4½"h; reverse has, "Season The World With The Gospel"; it is reported that matching salt and pepper shakers rest on small platforms; C; $150.00 – 175.00.

Plate 906. World globe, same as #54 except 3"h; C; $150.00 – 200.00.

Plate 907. Drum, porcelain, ca. 1925, Germany; C; $175.00 – 225.00.

Plate 908. Telephone, pottery, ca. 1925, US, 4⅜"h; Clemison's mark on back; B; $100.00 – 150.00.

ापार

Plate 909. Iron, same as #101 except overpaint, 5⅝"h; C; $100.00 – 125.00.

Plate 910. Alarm clock, same as #54 except 4⅜"h; D; $175.00 – 200.00.

Plate 911. Ornate clock, same as #54 except D; $175.00 – 200.00.

Plate 912. Clock over mantel, pottery, ca. 1910, English, 4⅛"h; E; $250.00 – 300.00.

Plate 913. Fireplace, pottery, ca. 1900, US(?); D; $175.00 – 200.00.

Plate 914. Cash register, same as #54 except comes in three sizes 4"h, 4¼"h, and 5¼"h; rated A, B, and C; $75.00 – 150.00.

Plate 915. One kilogram weight, pottery, ca. 1920(?), European; E; $150.00 – 200.00.

Plate 916. Safe, same as #54 except 3⅜"h, without store ad; B; $100.00 – 125.00; with store ad (as shown); D; $175.00 – 200.00.

Plate 917. Victorian box, same as #54(?) except D; $175.00 – 200.00.

Plate 918. Money Box, pottery (majolica?), ca. 1860, English; probably the early product from whence money boxes derived their name; E; $200.00 – 225.00.

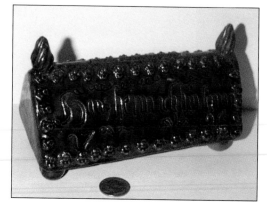

Plate 919. Fancy box, pottery, 1796, German, 4"h; "Hanshemniefhm 1796" inscribed; F; $350.00 – 400.00.

Plate 920. Folding money box, pottery, (majolica?), ca. 1850, English; D; $200.00 – 225.00.

Plate 921. Flowered money pot, pottery, ca. 1900, European, 3"h; C; $150.00 – 175.00.

Plate 922. Piano, same as #54 except 4¼"h; B; $125.00 – 150.00.

Plate 923. Heater, porcelain, ca. 1910, Germany, 3"h; D; $150.00 – 175.00.

Plate 924. Basket of flowers, pottery, ca. 1920, European; D; $175.00 – 200.00.

Plate 925. Mail box, porcelain, ca. 1920, German, 3⅛"h; C; $140.00 – 160.00.

Plate 926. Mail box, same as #54 except scarce blue color, 3¾"h, without store ad; B; $85.00 – 110.00; with store ad (as shown), D; $175.00 – 200.00.

Plate 927. Round mail box, porcelain, ca. 1920, European(?); D; $175.00 – 200.00.

Plate 928. Merry Xmas bell, same as #54 except 3¾"h; C; $125.00 – 150.00.

Plate 929. 1936 Olympic bell, porcelain, ca. 1935, German, 4"h; cross collected by Olympic and Nazi collectors; D; $400.00 – 500.00.

Plate 930. Stein, same as #54 except 3¾"h, without store ad; B; $100.00 – 125.00; with store ad (as shown); C; $150.00 – 175.00.

Plate 931. Cup, same as #54 except 2¼"h; "Bank of Deposits" inscribed around body; B; $90.00 – 110.00.

Plate 932. Van Dyke teapot, same as #144 except 3¼"h; Van Dyke Teas advertising usually on bottom; A; $50.00 – 75.00.

Plate 933. Jasperware teapot, blue and white jasperware (usually called Wedgwood after its most famous producer) pottery, ca. 1910, European (not Wedgwood), 4"h; C; $200.00 – 250.00.

Plate 934. Jasperware sugar bowl, see #933, except 3½"h; D; $300.00 – 350.00.

Plate 935. Lion footed dresser, scroddleware pottery, ca. 1850, US, Philadelphia, Pa. Herr Pottery 5½"h (Breininger collection); two sizes, difficult to find without damage; D; $300.00 – 350.00.

Plate 936. Primitive dresser, heavy pottery, ca. 1820, English, 5½"h; E; $300.00 – 350.00.

Plate 937. Twisted edge dresser, pottery, ca. 1900, English, 2¾"h; B; $75.00 – 110.00.

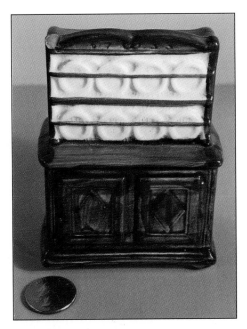

Plate 938. China cabinet, same as #191 except 4½"h; D; $225.00 – 275.00.

Plate 939. Rolled top desk, same as #54 except 3½"h; D; $200.00 – 225.00.

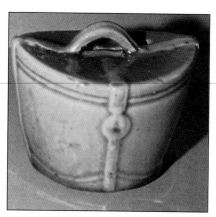

Plate 940. Carrying tub, same as #54 except 2½"h; a larger one by the FCP exists with the handle flat on top, same rating; C; $125.00 – 150.00.

Plate 941. Stump with leaves, same as #54 except D; $175.00 – 200.00.

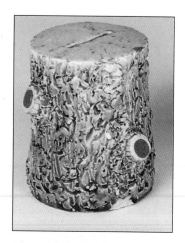

Plate 942. Stump, pottery, ca. 1910, US(?); D; $175.00 – 200.00.

Plate 943. Plymouth Rock, redware, ca. 1910, US, Washamein Pottery, Sterling, MO, 3"h; C; $125.00 – 150.00.

Purses, Satchels, Suitcases, Trunks & Money Bags

Plate 944. Plain purse, same as #144 except porcelain colored version, 3"h; AUSTRIA raised strip on back; D; $175.00 – 200.00.

Plate 945. Purse with flower, porcelain, ca. 1925, Germany, 2⅝"h; C; $140.00 – 180.00.

Plate 946. Fat purse, pottery, ca. 1920, US(?), 1⅝"h; D; $175.00 – 200.00.

Plate 947. Motto purse, pottery, ca. 1910, Scotland, 2¼"h; D; $175.00 – 200.00.

Plate 948. Lumpy purse, heavy pottery, ca. 1880, England, 2½"h; E; $225.00 – 250.00.

Plate 949. Elegant purse, porcelain, ca. 1910, Germany(?), 2½"h; D; $200.00 – 250.00.

Plate 950. Souvenir satchel, porcelain, ca. 1930, England, 2⅝"h; C; $125.00 – 150.00.

Plate 951. Plain satchel, pottery, ca. 1920, US, 2⅜"h; souvenir, Seattle, Was. barely visible; C; $100.00 – 125.00.

Plate 952. Rope handle satchel, same as #54 except 2⅛"h; C; $125.00 – 150.00.

Plate 953. Doctor's satchel, same as #54 except 2½"h; C; $125.00 – 150.00.

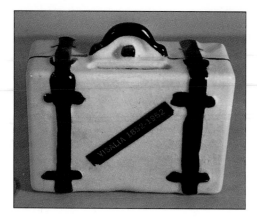

Plate 954. Strapped suitcase, pottery, ca. 1940 (and later), US, 3⅛"h; B; $65.00 – 80.00.

Plate 955. Plain suitcase, same as #54 except 2¾"h; B; $85.00 – 110.00.

Plate 956. Trunk, same as #54 except 2¼"h; B; $85.00 – 110.00.

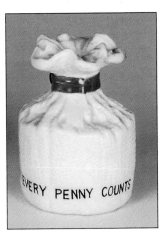

Plate 957. Every Penny Counts moneybag, porcelain(?), ca. 1920, European; C; $100.00 – 125.00.

Plate 958. Dollar sign moneybag, same as #101 except 4⅝"h; B; $75.00 – 90.00.

Plate 959. Seamed moneybag, pottery, ca. 1910, European, 4"h; D; $150.00 – 175.00.

Plate 960. 100,000 moneybag, porcelain, ca. 1920, Germany, 3¼"h; C; $125.00 – 150.00.

Plate 961. Well tied moneybag, pottery, ca. 1860, US(?), 3¾"h; E; $200.00 – 275.00.

Plate 962. 1,000 moneybag, same as #54 except D; $175.00 – 200.00.

Glossary

The best source for ceramic terms is *An Illustrated Dictionary of Ceramics* (3,054 terms) by George Savage and Harold Newman, Thames & Hudson, 500 Fifth Ave., NY, NY 11110, it was still in print at this writing.

Artificial porcelain — or soft paste porcelain is made using powdered glass instead of feldspathic rock to create the translucency and is fused at 1200° F.

Bisque (also called Bisquit) — unglazed pottery or porcelain that has only been fired once.

Bohemia — one of three sections of modern Czechoslovakia (1918 – 1990) carved from the former Austro-Hungarian empire following WWI. A long-time center of Eastern European ceramics manufacturing.

Bone china porcelain — a true porcelain, adds bone ash obtained from animal bones which improves the fusion of the ingredients and is otherwise like hard paste porcelain.

Ceramic — is used to describe all fired products using some earth-mined clays.

Clay — earth whose essential component is hydrous aluminum silicate which keeps it plastic. It retains shape as it drys but can be made plastic again by addition of water. Once heated or fired above 450° centigrade it becomes permanently hard.

Coloring Room — the place within a ceramic factory where various colors, glazes, and other chemicals used in the production, glazing, and finishing of ceramics are stored and mixed for use.

Crazing or Crackle Finish — a series of minute surface cracks in the glaze of ceramics usually induced by different cooling rates of the ceramic and the glaze.

Drain Mold — the ceramic is poured into it in a liquid state with fast setting chemicals added. A thin layer on the outside quickly forms and the excess liquid clay is drained through a hole in the bottom and used for the next pieces. The drain hole is sometimes plugged.

Earthenware — contains primarily earth-mined clays and is further divided into pottery and stoneware.

FCP — four color pottery, a prolific ceramic banks maker in the Bohemian province of the Austro-Hungarian Empire before 1917.

Footed — indicates an edge around bottom of a ceramic piece on which the piece rests.

Glaze — is the substance applied over the decoration and ceramic body. Glazing is applied before, after, or during firing. If applied after, it requires refiring. It is usually applied in a liquid or powder form. In most cases it produces a glass-like waterproof, durable, and attractive finish.

Green ceramic or ware — unfired. Firing reduces size by 17%.

Hard-Paste Porcelain — true porcelain which contains white refractory clay or kaolin and feldspathic rock. It fuses at over 1450° F.

HEPP — hole-eyed pottery pigs made in Bohemia province of the Austro-Hungarian Empire, or Czechoslovakia after 1917.

Jasper ware — a hard, fine grained unglazed stoneware (invented by Sir Thomas Wedgwood and often called Wedgwood). Jasper ware has been made by many companies besides Wedgwood since its introduction in 1774.

MAJ — the prolific majolica coin bank manufacturer of post 1917 Czechoslovakia.

Majolica — one of the most collected and appreciated of the earthenware potteries, originally a cheap competitor to porcelain. It is also called Maiolica (if Italian where it originated), Delftware (Holland), faience (France), mezza-maiolica, and raffaele ware. Majolica (a trade name used by Minton in Staffordshire area) is a tin glazed bright and colorful earthenware.

Molding, Hand — is the oldest method and is forming the clay shape with the hands before firing.

Ohr, George — the most famous American art potter.

Overpaint (also called overglaze and on glaze) — painting on a glazed piece, usually then refired at a lower temperature to set the paint.

Pastille (Burners) — pastille is an aromatic or medicated paste for burning, a popular nineteenth century activity. Many Staffordshire money boxes are adapted from pastille burners or vice versa.

Porcelain — is a translucent ceramic and/or gives a ringing note when struck. There are three general types; hard paste, soft paste (or artificial china), and bone china. Porcelain is made by combining fusible minerals, usually feldspar, with clay.

Porcelain, hard paste — a true porcelain, contains white refractory clay or Kaolin and feldspathic rock. It fuses at over 1450° F.

Porcelain, soft paste or artificial — see Artificial Porcelain.

"Potteries, The" — The Staffordshire area in mid-northwest England comprising Stoke-on-Trent, Tunstall, Hanley, Burslem, Longdon, and Fenton. Also known as the five towns (there are six) and the Staffordshire area. Many major potteries are located there.

Pottery — earth-mined clay ranging from open fire heated to kiln heated at 800° degrees F or higher. Requires glazing for waterproofing. It scratches easily.

Presentation Bank — one made for a particular person usually with their name or initials and/or an important date, usually their birthday.

Press Mold — the green ceramic is pressed into the hollow mold cavity until it hardens sufficiently to remove. Where there were mold seams a seam remains and is usually smoothed out with excess ceramic removed. The care of finishing the seam is often a clue to the quality of the piece.

Roseville — large and venerable ceramic manufacturer located in Roseville and Zanesville, Ohio, from 1885 to 1954, who produced a substantial number of coin banks beginning in the 1890s.

Scrodled ware — layers of different colored clays wedged together to make random patterns like chocolate and vanilla ice cream mixed together.

Sgraffito — decoration made by scoring a design through slip applied to the piece before glazing to reveal the clay beneath.

Stoneware — made of clay and fusible stone usually heated above 1000° F. There are several subcategories which are of little interest since there are few stoneware banks. Is heavy and difficult to scratch.

Wheel-turned pottery — is pottery formed on a potter's wheel and is always cylindrical.

Bibliography

Andacht, Sandra, Nancy Garth, and Robert Mascarelli. *Price Guide to Oriental Antiques.* West Des Moines, IA: Wallace-Homestead, 1984.

Barret, Richard Carter. *Bennington Pottery & Porcelain.* New York, NY: Bonanza Books, 1958.

Bemrose, Geoffrey. *Nineteenth Centure English Pottery and Porcelain.* London, England: Faber and Faber, 1952.

Clark, Ellison & Hecht. *The Mad Potter of Biloxi — The Life & Art of George E. Ohr.* New York, NY: Abbville Press, 1989.

Clark, Garth. *A Century of Ceramics in the United States 1878 – 1978.* New York, NY: E.P. Dutton, 1979.

Cox, Warren E. *The Book of Pottery and Porcelain, Vol. I.* New York, NY: Crown Publishers, Inc., 1970.

Dawes, Nicholas M. *Majolica.* New York, NY: Crown Publishers, Inc., 1990.

Duer, Don. *A Penny Saved.* Atglen, PA: Schiffer Publishing Ltd., 1993.

Emmerling, Mary Ellisor. *Collecting American Country.* New York, NY: Clarkson N. Potter, Inc. 1983.

Evans, Paul. *Art Pottery of the United States.* New York, NY: Feingold & Lewis Publishing Corp., 1960.

Forsyth, Ruth A. *Made in Czechoslovakia — Book 2.* Marietta, OH: The Glass Press, Inc., 1993.

Guilland, Harold F. *The Early American Folk Pottery.* Philadelphia, PA: Chilton Book Co., 1971.

Hammond, Dorothy. *Mustache Cups.* Des Moines, IA: Wallace-Homestead Book Co., 1972.

Huxfords. *Collector's Encyclopedia of Roseville Pottery Vo. 1 & 2.* Paducah, KY: Collector Books, 1986.

Index of Collectable Penny Banks. Compiled and published by the members of the Still Bank Collectors Club of America, layout by Maxine Goldberg, indexed by Blossom Abell, word processing by Florence Clayton, 1982.

Jobes, Gertrude. *Dictionary of Mythology Folklore and Symbols.* New York, NY: The Scarecrow Press, Inc., 1961 – 1963.

Johnson, Deb and Gini. *Beginner's Book of American Pottery.* Des Moines, IA: Wallace-Homestead Book Co., 1974.

Jordan, Charles & Donna. *The Official Price Guide to Pottery & Porcelain.* New York, NY: The House of Collectibles, 1986.

Joya, Mock. *Things Japanese.* Tokyo, Japan: Tokyo News Service, Ltd., 1960.

Kenny, John B. *Ceramic Sculpture.* Philadelphia, PA: Chilton Book Company, 1953 (rec 1971).

Ketchum, William C. *American Country Pottery.* New York, NY: Alfred A. Knopf, 1987.

_____. *American Redware.* New York, NY: Henry Holt and Company, 1991.

_____. *American Stoneware.* New York, NY: Henry Holt and Company, 1991.

_____. *Pottery & Porcelain.* New York, NY: Alfred A. Knopf, 1983.

Kovel, Ralph M. and Terry H. *Dictionary of Marks — Pottery and Porcelain.* New York, NY: Crown Publishers, 1953.

Lau, Theodora. *Handbook of Chinese Horoscopes*. New York, NY: Harper & Row, 1979.

Lewis, Griselda. *A Collector's History of English Pottery*. New York, NY: Harper & Row, 1979.

_____. *A Picture History of English Pottery*. London, England: Hulton Press, 1976.

Long, Earnest and Ida, and Jane Pitman. *Dictionary of Still Banks*. Mokelumne Hille, CA: Long's Americana, 1980.

McCaslin, Mary J. *Royal Bayreuth: A Collector's Guide*. Marietta, OH: The Glass Press, Inc., 1994.

McConnell, Kevin. *Redware America's Folk Art Pottery*. West Chester, PA: Schiffer Publishing Ltd., USA, 1988.

Moore, Andy & Susan. *The Penny Bank Book*. Exton, PA: Schiffer Publishing Ltd., 1984.

Morley-Fletcher, Hugo. *Meissen Porcelain in Color*. New York, NY: Exeter Books, 1979.

New Encyclopedia Britannica, the, USA. Chicago, IL: The Encyclopedia Britannica, 1768, 15th Edition, 1987.

Pennington, Samuels; Thomas M. Vass; Lita Solis-Cohen. *Americana at Auction*, 1978.

Ramsay, John. *American Potters and Pottery*. Boston, MA: Hale, Cushman & Flint, 1939.

Ramsey, L.G.G. *The Connoisseur New Guide to Antique English Potter, Porcelain, and Glass*. New York, NY: E.P. Dutton & Company, Inc., 1961.

Sandon, Henry: *Coffee Pots and Teapots*. New York, NY: Arco Publishing Co., Inc., 1974.

Savage, George and Harold Newman. *An Illustrated Dictionary of Ceramics*. London, England: Thames and Hudson, 1974, rev. 1985.

Seaman's Bank for Savings (The). *Christie's Mechanical and Still Banks Sold on Behalf of the F.D.I.C.* New York, NY: March 3, 1991.

Schneider, Mike. *Majolica*. West Chester, PA: Schiffer Publishing Ltd., 1990.

Schwartz, Marvin D. *Collectors' Guide to Antique American Ceramics*. Garden City, NY: Doubleday & Co., 1969.

Shull, Thelma. *Victorian Antiques*. Rutland, VT: Charles E. Tuttle Co., 1963.

Spargo, John. *The Potters and Potteries of Bennington*. New York, NY: Dover Publications, Inc., 1926 & 1972.

Stitt, Irene. *Japanese Ceramics of the Last 100 Years*. New York, NY: Crown Publishers, Inc., 1974.

Thurn, Hans Peter. *Die Kultur der Sparsamkeit*. Deutcher Stuttgart, Germany: Sparkassenverlag GmbH, 1982.

About the Authors

Tom Stoddard

Graduated San Francisco State University majoring in philosophy — also has done post graduate work and attended Long Beach City College, Yuba College, College of Marin, and USAF Cadet School; former government official and vice president of Wells Fargo Bank.

Authored following published material:

Numerous jazz articles and biographies published in *Coda* (Canada), *IAJRC Journal* (U.S.), and *Storyville* (England).

Book: *Pops Foster — The Autobiography of a New Orleans Jazzman.* University of California Press, Berkeley, CA. (Winner of 1972 ASCAP award.)

Book: *Jazz on the Barbary Coast.* Storyville Press, London, England.

Book: *Computer Cleanout.* Barlow Press, Cotati, California, 1993.

Tom Stoddard's book of miscellaneous writings, *Computer Cleanout* (a compendium of essays, aphorisms, short stories, and diatribes) is available from him for $5 plus $2 packing and shipping in the US. Send orders to Tom Stoddard, PO Box 71, Petaluma, CA 94953.

Numerous articles, short stories, and a column on wilderness, wildlife, conservation, and the environment in *Earth First! Journal.*

Numerous articles on still and mechanical coin banks which have appeared in the *Penny Post*, *The Mechanical Banker,* and *Antique Toy World.* Currently one of the best known researcherwriters on still and mechanical coin banks.

Tom began collecting coin banks in 1988, and quickly focused on the beauty of ceramic coin banks. He also discovered little was known or printed about them. To fill this void he began extensive research and has written a number of articles about them. His research and material have grown into this book. He is a member Mechanical Bank Collectors of America and Still Bank Collectors Club of America (SBCCA Director 1990 – 1992). Collects all types of pre-WWII still and mechanical banks, maintaining the largest pre-WWII ceramic bank collection in the world.

Loretta Stoddard

Obtained BA and MA from San Francisco State University in business education. Has held teaching positions at Diablo Valley College and Heald College. Currently an instructor at College of Marin, Marin County, California, in the business department. Teaches a variety of business subjects including computer applications. Has written numerous training materials used in the computer classes.

Photographs various small antiques including coin banks. Coin bank photographs have been published in *Antique Toy World*, *The Penny Post,* and *The Mechanical Banker.*

Other interests include traveling, gardening, and collecting antiques (especially old restaurant creamers with names and children's sewing machines).

Has a keen eye for finding banks for Tom and has done most of the hard work of reading, correcting, and reviewing text.

Index

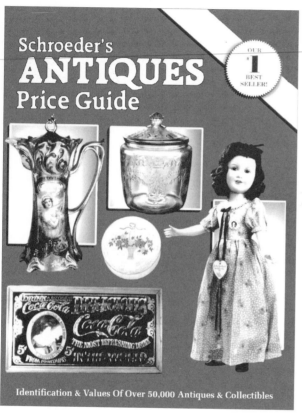